ORACLE OF GOD
DEVOTIONAL

JULY - DEC

Stevie Okauru

MARK ASEMOTA
House of publishing

Mark Asemota House of Publishing
535 Pensacola Dr
Gaithersburg, Md 20878

Ordering Information:
Quantity sales. Special discounts are available on quantity
purchases by corporations, associations, and others. For details,
contact the publisher at the address above.
Orders by U.S. trade bookstores and wholesalers.
Please contact Big Distribution:
P. O. BOX 14068 RALEIGH NC 27620.
TEL: 1800.481.3884. FAX: 1888.413.5990

Printed in the United States of America

Publisher's Cataloging-in-Publication data
Stevie Okauru.

ISBN 978-0-9883448-9-1

First Edition

This Gift is
Presented to

_____

_____

_____

BY

_____

_____

_____

CUP
OF THE
LORD

STEVIE OKAURU ©

THE WORD IS ALIVE IN ME

In the name of Jesus, God's Word is alive; it is alive in me. God speaks to me through His Word; He gives me revelation through His Word. I accept His Word and act upon it accordingly. God's Word is true, I believe it. I walk in the light of what the Word says, because the Word of God is God speaking to me. The word of God works for me as I obediently work for it.

BY GRACE I RECEIVED THE RIGHTEOUSNESS OF CHRIST JESUS

Jesus became sin so I might be righteous in the eyes of God. I am the righteousness of God in Christ. I have received the gift of righteousness, which puts me in good standing with God. I reign in life because I am righteous and God hears me when I pray. My prayers avail much. I know that righteousness is not sinlessness, but in right standing with God. I know that I am saved by faith through Jesus Christ. Not by my works, but by the finished work of Jesus Christ on the cross of Calvary.

*"If any man speak, **let him speak as the oracles of God**; if any man minister, let him do it as of the ability which God giveth: that God in all things may be glorified through Jesus Christ, to whom be praise and dominion for ever and ever. Amen."*

1 Peter 4:11 (KJV)

July 1ˢᵗ

THE WORD TODAY: Psalm 103:1 (KJV)

"Bless the Lord, O my soul: and all that is within me bless his holy name."

𝒟avid said: Bless the Lord O my soul and all that is within me bless His Holy Name. Bless the Lord O my soul and forget not all His benefits. Human memory can be very short, particularly when it comes to good things. We tend to remember bad things more. If a man begins to weep, three years after his wife died, everyone will say, O see how he so loved his wife. But if he continues to shout and praise God three months after his wife had a baby, people will ask that he be taken to a psychiatric hospital. Saint! Don't be like the world. Don't quickly forget what the Lord has done for you. Remember all He did for you last year, remember what He's done for you since the beginning of this year, since you became born again. Remember what He's done for you since you were an infant. Remember how many of you went to elementary school together. Remember how many of them are gone now. Remember the mercies of God! Don't forget all His benefits. Give Him the glory He deserves and worship Jehovah! Go ahead and bless the Lord! Bless the Lord O my soul and all that is within me bless His Holy Name. Forget not all His benefits! Don't forget His healings! Don't forget all His deliverances! Don't forget His victories of the past! Bless Him! Praise Him! Worship Him! Remember all He has done for you! Count your blessings! Count them one by one! Remember all His goodness! All His mercy! All His faithfulness! Forget not all His benefits – how many times you escaped from accident; how many times you slept and you woke up! The enemy didn't want you to wake up but you woke up! Give God all the glory, all the honor and adoration, for He is the King of Glory! Alleluia!

July 02ⁿᵈ

The Word Today: Ecclesiastes 7:8

THE 2ND PART OF THIS YEAR WILL BE BETTER THAN THE 1ST!

This is the 2nd day of the 2nd half of this year. This is a time for reflection, a time to re-evaluate whether the goals that you set for the year have been achieved or are still pending in any way. When goals are not yet achieved, there is the tendency of anxiety and fear. That is why the end of each year, is usually a time of desperation for many people. But for those who know and do God's word, it is not so. According to our text-verse above, the end of a thing is supposed to be better than the beginning. The end should be a time of rejoicing, joy and happiness and not a time of anxiety and fear. That is why believers need not panic at any time of their lives. It is also based on that principle that I now, decree unto you that the second half of this year will be greater and better for you in Jesus' name. Amen! Have you had any success so far this year? If yes, then prepare for greater success because the best is yet to come. But if you have not had a good report thus far, then prepare for a better season coming because your year will be crowned with good success and abundance of goodness in Jesus' name. Amen! All you need to do is accept this word of prophecy and continually declare it in your life and it is done! As you do so, in every area of your life, in your marriage, your finances, career, and business, health, and wealth, physically and spiritually, expect a turnaround breakthrough! Instead of being anxious, it would be more rewarding for you to be expectant and hopeful. And the remaining part of this year will be better for you than the beginning in Jesus' name!

Prayer: *Lord! Let the second half of this year be better for me!*

3

The Word Today: 1 Thessalonians 5:17-18 (Amp)

"Be unceasing in prayer [praying perseveringly] Thank [God] in everything....

I WILL ENCOUNTER GOD'S GOODNESS THIS TIME!

We must live by faith for the scriptures say the just shall live by faith. God is working everything together for good for us, no matter what our situation may be right now. And as we respond to God with gratitude, He will lift and promote us physically and spiritually to a new and greater altitude. As we appreciate God, we will see the fruition of our expectations. We would experience oneness and wholeness with the Holy Spirit; fellowship with the Holy Spirit becomes a reality. We would then receive supernatural deliverance from whatever demonic captivity we are trapped in. This was the attitude of Paul and Silas in Acts 16:16-26. Are you in captivity of poverty? Are you living from pay check to pay check? Is it a court case, sickness, Joblessness, loneliness, singleness or bareness that has stolen your peace? God has a solution for you this day. Go ahead and thank Him now and see how things will positively turn around for you in Jesus' name. Amen!

PRAYER OF THANKSGIVING!

Thank You Almighty God! Glory to Your Holy Name! King of Kings and Lord of Lords I bless Your Holy name. Thank You for Your goodness and mercy! Thank You for Your support and faithfulness! I thank You O Lord from the bottom of my heart! I give You all glory, honor and adoration! Thank You for loving and saving my soul! Thank You for keeping me and my loved ones alive! If I have a thousand tongues it is not enough to thank You! Father Thank You. Accept my thanks in Jesus' name. Amen!

The Word Today: James 4:2-3

".......Yet you do not have because you do not ask. You ask and do not receive, because you ask amiss, that you may spend it on your pleasures."

I PROPHESY! I WILL NO MORE ASK AMISS!

*D*evastating things continue unabated in our lives, such as marital distress, stubborn sickness, generational poverty, overwhelming fear and confusion. We continue to suffer all these afflictions and infirmities because we do not pray enough or pray aright. All the harassment and embarrassment from the kingdom of darkness are actually self-inflicted wounds, and they don't have to continue if we stop praying amiss. And start praying right.

In spite of what's going on with the economy of the world, those who learn how to access heaven with their prayers will always share powerful testimonies. There are prayers that work in good times as well as in bad times. Elijah prayed fervently and effectually during famine and had abundant rain. 1 Kings Chapters 17 and 18; James 5:16-18 he prayed a prayer of faith. King Solomon did not ask amiss in abundance. 2 Chronicles 1:11. There are prayers that can overcome and overthrow all hindrances, barriers and roadblocks. But like anything that's worthwhile, it takes training and spiritual discipline to pray aright. For instance many believers may read this and just nod, smile and then tuck it away and do nothing! But others will read this script, take everything to heart, and begin to pray... starting right away. If you belong to the later group, I congratulate you. And I prophesy you will never again pray amiss in Jesus' name!

Prayer: *Lord! Enable me to pray aright in Jesus' name. Amen!*

WORD SWORD OF THE ORACLE

The Word Today: Genesis 1:1 (NKJV)

---

*"In the beginning **God** created the heavens and the earth."*

GOD [HEBREW] *ELOHIM*

The Hebrew word for God is *Elohim [Strong Creator]* as used in Genesis 1:1, Genesis 1:26, Deuteronomy 7:9, and Isaiah 45:18 Strong's #430. "El" the short form of Elohim is found 250 times in the Bible. And this is the traditional Hebrew term for God. This word is relative to similar words used for deity in most Semitic languages. It means "Mighty". In Hebrew Elohim, The Almighty frequently occurs in the plural sense of the word. *[The Plural of Majesty]* which is, in great contrast to the normal gods of the heathen: - Like the false gods in 1 Kings 19:2. The Hebrews uses this Plural not to really mean multiple deity but "The fullness of Majesty of the Deity God Almighty" Meaning "The very God." Many Believers agree to the plural form of this word as to revealing the plurality of the Godhead and nature of God. God is One and He is also three distinct person in the Trinity; The Father! The Son! And The Holy Spirit.

Here are some names of God:

List of the Names of GOD the Father in the Old Testament

1. Elohim-GOD Genesis 1:1 -The strong creator.

2. Jehovah-LORD Genesis 2:4 -The self-existing One.

3. Adonai-LORD/Master Genesis 15:2-The Headship.

The Compound Names

"The LORD GOD "Jehovah El and Jehovah Elohim"

1. Jehovah El Elohim Joshua 22:22-The LORD GOD of GODS.

2. Jehovah Elohim Genesis 2:4, 3:9-13, 21- The LORD GOD.

3. Jehovah Elohe Abothekem Joshua 18:3- The LORD GOD of your fathers

4. Jehovah El Elyon Genesis 14:22- The LORD, the Most High God

5. Jehovah El Emeth Psalms 31:5- LORD GOD of Truth.

6. Jehovah El Gemuwal Jeremiah 51:56 The LORD GOD of recompenses

7. Jehovah Elohim Tsebaoth Psalms 59:5, Isaiah 28:22- LORD GOD of Hosts.

8. Jehovah Elohe Yeshuathi Psalms 88:1- LORD GOD of my salvation.

9. Jehovah Elohe Yisrael Psalms 41:13- The LORD GOD of Israel.

The Compound Names GOD "El, Elohim, and Elohe"

1. **Elohim** Genesis 1:1 GOD

2. **Elohim Bashamayim** Joshua 2:11- GOD in Heaven.

3. **El Bethel** (Genesis 35:7) - GOD of the House of GOD.

4. **Elohe Chaseddi** Psalms 59:10- The GOD of My Mercy.

5. **Elohe Yisrael** Genesis 33:20- GOD, the GOD of Israel.

Someone once said "They that walk; walks with the multitude. They that run runs with a few and they that fly, fly's alone". And then somebody added "If you want to be among the many, all you need is common sense, you don't have tothink before you walk. If you want to run with the few you need advice but if you want to fly you need instruction. That is why those who teach pilots to fly are called flight instructors.

Are you *ready* *to fly?*

then be instructed!

Stevie Okauru, the Oracle of God.
Founder & Senior Pastor
ORACLE OF GOD INTERNATIONAL MINISTRIES INC.
An International Full Gospel and Deliverance Prayer Ministry
www.oogod.org/ pastor@oogod.org

6. **El Elyon** .Gen. 14:18, Dan. 3:26, Psalms 78:56- The Most High GOD.

7. **El Emunah** Deuteronomy 7:9- The Faithful GOD.

8. **El Gibbor** Isaiah 9:6- Mighty GOD.

9. **El Hakabodh** Psalms 29:3- The GOD of Glory.

10. **El Hay** Joshua 3:10, Jeremiah 23:36, Daniel 3:26- The Living GOD.

11. **El Hayyay** Psalms 42:8- GOD of My Life.

12. **Elohim Kedoshim** Joshua 24:19- Holy GOD.

13. **El Kanna** Exodus 20:5- Jealous GOD.

14. **El Kanno** Joshua 24:19- Jealous GOD.

15. **Elohe Mauzi** Psalms 43:2- GOD of My Strength.

16. **Elohim Machase Lanu** Psalms 62:8- GOD Our Refuge.

17. **Eli Maelekhi** Psalms 68:24- GOD My King.

18. **El Marom** Micah 6:6 - GOD Most High.

19. **El Nekamoth** Psalms 18:47 - GOD that Avengeth.

20. **El Nose** Psalms 99:8- GOD that Forgave.

21. **Elohenu Olam** Psalms 48:14- Our Everlasting GOD.

22. **Elohim Ozer Li** Psalms 54:4- GOD My Helper.

23. **El Rai** Genesis 16:13- GOD Seest Me.

24. **Elsali** Psalms 42:9- GOD, My Rock.

25. **El Shaddai** Genesis 17:1-2, Ezekiel 10:5- Almighty GOD.

8

26. **Elohim Shophtim Ba-arets** Ps. 58:11 GOD that Judgeth in the Earth.

27. **El Simchath Gili** Psalms 43:4- GOD My Exceeding Joy.

28. **Elohim Tsebaoth** Ps. 80:7, Jer. 35:17, Jer. 38:17- GOD of Hosts.

29. **Elohe Tishuathi** Psalms 18:46, Psalm 51:14- GOD of My Salvation.

30. **Elohe Tsadeki** Psalms 4:1 - GOD of My Righteousness.

31. **Elohe Yakob** Psalms 20:1 - GOD of Israel.

32. **Elohe Yisrael** Psalms 59:5- GOD of Israel.

The Compound Name Jehovah

1. **Jehovah** Exodus 6:2-3- The LORD.

2. **Adonai Jehovah** Genesis 15:2- Lord GOD.

3. **Jehovah Adon Kol Ha-arets** Joshua 3:11- The LORD, the Lord of all the earth

4. **Jehovah Bore** Isaiah 40:28- The LORD Creator.

5. **Jehovah Chereb** Deuteronomy 33:29- The LORD... the Sword.

6. **Jehovah Eli** Psalms 18:2- The LORD My GOD.

7. **Jehovah Elyon** Genesis 14:18-20- The LORD Most High.

8. **Jehovah Gibbor Milchamah** Psalms 24:8- The LORD Mighty In Battle.

9. **Jehovah Maginnenu** Psalms 89:18- The LORD Our Defense.

10. **Jehovah Goelekh** Is. 49:26, Is. 60:16- The LORD Thy Redeemer.

11. **Jehovah Hashopet** Judges 11:27- The LORD the Judge.

12. **Jehovah Hoshiah** Psalms 20:9- O LORD Save.

13. **Jehovah Immeka** Judges 6:12- The LORD Is with You.

14. **Jehovah Izuz Wegibbor** Psalms 24:8- The LORD Strong and Mighty.

15. **Jehovah-jireth** Genesis 22:14- The LORD Shall Provide.

16. **Jehovah Kabodhi** Psalms 3:3- The LORD My GOD.

17. **Jehovah Kanna Shemo** Exodus 34:14 - The LORD Whose Name Is Jealous.

18. **Jehovah Keren-Yishi** Psalms 18:2- The LORD the Horn of My Salvation.

19. **Jehovah Machsi** Psalms 91:9- The LORD My Refuge.

20. **Jehovah Magen** Deuteronomy 33:29- The LORD the Shield.

21. **Jehovah Makkeh** Ezekiel 7:9- The LORD that Smiteth.

22. **Jehovah Mauzzam** Psalms 37:39- The LORD Their Strength.

23. **Jehovah Mauzzi** Jeremiah 16:19- The LORD My Fortress.

24. **Ha-Melech Jehovah** Psalms 98:6 - The LORD the King.

25. **Jehovah Melech Olam** Psalms 10:16- The LORD King Forever.

26. **Jehovah Mephalti** Psalms 18:2- The LORD My Deliverer.

27. **Jehovah Mekaddishkem** Ex. 31:13- The LORD that Sanctifies You.

28. **Jehovah Metsudhathi** Psalms 18:2 - The LORD My High Tower.

29. **Jehovah Moshiekh** Is. 49:26 Is. 60:16- The LORD Your Savior.

30. **Jehovah Nissi** Exodus 17:15- The LORD My Banner.

31. **Jehovah Ori** Psalms 27:1- The LORD My Light.

32. **Jehovah Uzzi** Psalms 28:7- The LORD My Strength.

33. **Jehovah Rophe** Exodus 15:26- The LORD (our) Healer.

34. **Jehovah Roi** Psalms 23:1- The LORD My Shepherd.

35. **Jehovah Sabaoth** Tsebaoth 1 Samuel 1:3- The LORD of Hosts.

36. **Jehovah Sali** Psalms 18:2- The LORD My Rock.

37. **Jehovah Shalom** Judges 6:24- The LORD (our) Peace.

38. **Jehovah Shammah** Ezekiel 48:35- The LORD Is There.

39. **Jehovah Tsidkenu** Jeremiah 23:6- The LORD Our Righteousness.

40. **Jehovah Tsuri** Psalms 19:14- O LORD My Strength.

There are three primary names of GOD in the OT; GOD (Elohim), LORD (Jehovah, or Yahweh), and LORD/Master (Adonai). And, GOD is called by over one hundred other compound names or descriptive titles."

Prayer:

1. *God Reveal Yourself to me in Jesus' name. Amen!*
2. *Holy Spirit refill me afresh in the name of Jesus!*
3. *Thank You Lord Jesus! For refilling me afresh! 1.Every anointing of destructive anger in my blood, dry up by fire, in the name of Jesus.*
4. *O Lord, deliver me from the spirit of ancestral anger in the name of Jesus.*

11

1st Sunday of the Month of July

CHURCH AND HOME SUNDAY SCHOOL

WHY DOES GOD THREATEN OUR INIQUITY UPON OUR CHILDREN?

*G*od threatens our iniquities on our children for us to fear the wrath of God: and flee from sin and not act contrary to His commandments. *"Therefore I will judge you, O house of Israel, every one according to his ways," says the Lord God. "Repent, and turn from all your transgressions, so that iniquity will not be your ruin."* Ezekiel 18:30 (NKJV)

HOW INIQUITY DOES DIFFERS FROM SIN?

WHAT IS INIQUITY?

Iniquity is the propensity to sin. It is the weakness within us which is a breeding ground for sin and it is in this area that the devil tempts us to transgress against God's laws. Especially in our mind. *"If Your Thinking is Stinky Your will be Sinking in Sin"*

WHAT IS SIN?

Sin is the willful and actual transgression and breaking of the laws of God. And transgression is trespassing, or exceeding the boundaries of our limits. *"Everyone who commits (practices) sin is guilty of lawlessness; for [that is what] sin is, lawlessness (the breaking, violating of God's law by transgression or neglect—being unrestrained and unregulated by His commands and His will)."* 1 John 3:4 (AMP)

"Behold, I was brought forth in iniquity, and in sin my mother conceived me." Psalm 51:5 (NKJV)

IF INQUITY IS ONLY THE BREEDING GROUND FOR SIN, WHY MUST WE BE FORGIVEN FOR THE SINS WE HAVE NOT COMMITED?

This is so, because God looks at the human heart, He knows our inward thoughts, intent and secret desires. Our heart must be pure before God; for it is the heart that condemns us.

"For every wrongdoer hates (loathes, detests) the Light, and will not come out into the Light but shrinks from it, lest his works (his deeds, his activities, his conduct) be exposed and reproved. But he who practices truth [who does what is right] comes out into the Light; so that his works may be plainly shown to be what they are—wrought with God [divinely prompted, done with God's help, in dependence upon Him]." John 3:20-21 (AMP)

"But I say to you that whoever looks at a woman to lust for her has already committed adultery with her in his heart." Matthew 5:28 (NKJV)

If I regard iniquity in my heart, The Lord will not hear." Psalm 66:18 (NKJV)

SUNDAY SCHOOL QUESTIONS

Q1. WHY DOES GOD THREATEN OUR INIQUITY UPON OUR CHILDREN? Q2. HOW DOES INIQUITY DIFFER FROM SIN? Q3. IF INQUITY IS ONLY THE BREEDING GROUND FOR SIN, WHY MUST WE BE FORGIVEN FOR THE SINS WE HAVE NOT COMMITED?

> **Memory Verse:** Psalm 66:18 *If I regard iniquity in my heart, the LORD will not hear.*

Prayer: *Merciful God have mercy upon me in Jesus' name. Amen!*

July 07th

The Word Today: Isaiah 12:4, Psalm 95:2-3

$\mathscr{B}$rethren, since we shouted Happy New Year six months ago, many people have died. Some died by road accident, some even were burnt to death. A whole family slept and they didn't wake up. We are not better or smarter than them; we are not holier or more righteous than them. Lamentations 3:22 says *"Through the Lord's mercies we are not consumed, because His compassions fail not."*

Saint; just go ahead and thank Him for His goodness! Thank Him for His preservation! Thank Him for Life! Thank Him for His mercies that endure forever! Thank Him for it is new every morning! Thank You Lord Jesus Christ! I Thank You for preservation! I am not in any way better, smarter or superior to people who are dead. It is by Your mercy O Lord that I am alive today! Thank You for January, February and March! Thank You for April, May and June! Thank You Lord for this month July! Thank You for I have seen the second half of this year. Thank You for protection and for provision! Thank You for Your love! Thank You for Your support! I give You all glory, honor and adoration! You're worthy to be praised! I Magnify Your Holy Name! I will praise You like never before. I thank You LORD for what You did for me in the past. Thank You for what You are doing now! Thank You for what You will yet do! I thank You from the bottom of my heart! Blessed be Your Holy Name LORD! Thank You Father in Jesus' mighty name. Amen!

URL: www.oogod.org/ E-Mail: *pastor@ oogod.org*

P. O. BOX 14068 RALEIGH NC 27620. TEL: 1800.481.3884. FAX: 1888.413.5990 PRAYERLINE: 267.507.0240 ENTER 605815 MONDAYS THROUGH SATURDAYS @ 6 AM AND 10 PM EST

The Word Today: Judges 2:11-16 [NIV]

"They were in great distress. Then the LORD rose up judges, who saved them out of the hands of these raiders."

I SHALL BE LIFTED UP BY THE MIGHTY HAND OF GOD!

*O*ne fact we must come to terms with is that there will always be challenges in life. Trials, temptations and tribulations etc., are all part of life's process of progression. There are always challenges for man at all times and they have their seasons. No wonder Job 14:1 [NIV] says *"Mortals, born of woman, are of few days and full of trouble."* Indeed life always throws challenges at us to raise us up and strong thereof. Our text-verses today support that theory. Each time the Jews disobeyed God, He made sure that they were kept in bondage [Judges 2:11-15]. Nevertheless, at the fullness of time, God always raised men/women [Judges] to deliver Israel from captivity. You become greater than the others when God chooses to use you for such deliverance from demonic bondages. Jephthah, Ehud, Samson, Gideon, Esther and Deborah etc., became great because God used them in such capacity to deliver people from their problems.

Do you desire to be used by God to deliver people from their issues? Listen Saint, problems are the processors of solutions. Just position yourself to be used to solve other people's problems to start with. Then change your mindset from impossibility to everything is possible. Begin to think of solutions instead of dwelling on the problems. And you will become a solution-[IST], a problem solver in Jesus' name!

Prayer: *LORD! Use me to solve problems that are around me!*

The Word Today: Psalm 100:1-4

MY ATTITUDE OF GRATITUDE WILL RAISE MY ALTITUDE IN LIFE!

Psalm 107:1-9 says "*O give thanks unto the LORD, for he is good: for his mercy endureth forever. Let the redeemed of the LORD say so, whom he hath redeemed them from the hand of the enemy; and gathered them out of the lands, from the east, and from the west, from the north, and from the south...... And he led them forth by the right way that they might go to a city of habitation. Oh that men would praise the LORD for his goodness, and for his wonderful works to the children of men! For He satisfied the longing soul, and filleth the hungry soul with goodness*".

Saint! Your attitude of gratitude is the determinant of your altitude in life. A grateful heart is a thankful heart. The elders say a grateful child will always receive more as they show appreciation for what they received in the past. You can't be joyful if you are not thankful and praise-full. So go ahead now and thank God for what He did for you in the past, so that He may do more for you today and in the future. Why not thank the Lord God almighty now and forever more!

PRAYER OF THANKS!

Lord, I thank You for what You did for me yesterday, last week, last month, last year and past years. Thank You for healings and deliverance, thank You for joy and breakthroughs, thank You for miracles, signs and wonders, thank You for salvation of souls, I bless Your Holy name, I give You all the glory and honor, thank You for what you are doing now and for what you will yet do in the future. Thank You Father! Thank You Lord Jesus! Blessed be Your Holy Name Lord in Jesus' gracious name I pray. Amen!

I SHALL RECEIVE A MAJOR BREAKTHROUGH!

All that we need in life, to succeed irreversibly, is one major breakthrough. One major breakthrough and we are settled for life. In Malachi 3:10 God said if you bring all the tithes into my house I will open the windows of heaven and pour you out a blessing, that there will not be enough room to receive it. One major breakthrough and suffering ends, poverty disappears. Even enemies will no longer be able to touch you and your loved ones because God will rebuke the devourer for your sake. In Luke 1:5-17 Elizabeth had a major breakthrough. She gave birth to only one son; but what a child! Jesus Christ said in Matthew 11:11 He said, of all men born of a woman, there had not arisen a greater man than John the Baptist. One child that surpassed all that had lived before him, one child that the world knew. I prophesy your testimony is going to shake the world!

In Mark 5:25-34 the woman with the issue of blood. She had been suffering for a long time. She was sick and had been going from one doctor to another draining her money. Doctors tried their best but failed. The tap refused to close! Every day, she grew weaker and poorer, her suffering and struggles multiplied but one day she had a major breakthrough! Just one contact with God! And that solved all her problems. I don't know what your own problems are. Whatever may have been draining your health and wealth, draining your strength, peace and joy: I decree, the power behind that issue is crushed in Jesus' name!

Prayer: *O God! Grant me a major breakthrough in Jesus' name!*

"......Behold, I lay in Zion for a foundation a stone, a tried stone, a precious corner stone, a sure foundation: he that believeth shall not make haste."

THE LORD GOD SHALL GRANT MY HEART'S DESIRE!

The following testimony will edify and increase your faith: "Praise the Lord! Praise the living Jesus! My name is Sister K. I thank the Lord that I am able to testify this day to the goodness of God in my life. In spite of all that the devil did to hinder me from giving my testimony; because I've been planning for days to do so, but I have being procrastinating. Since 2007 March my menstruation just stopped. I don't know what to do. I waited till maybe four to five months then I consulted my primary physician and then a gynecologist but nothing changed with all the medications and therapies. I discussed the issue with my twin sister, T. Who introduced me to the prayer conference of the Oracle of God Int'l ministries and from that very day I never missed a prayer session. One night, last month on the prayer conference Rev. Stevie said there is a woman here tonight whose menses have stopped for years now, the Lord said get a sanitary pad now for it will start to flow from tonight. I said Amen! And that night before I went to bed I used a sanitary pad by faith even though nothing was there. But to God be the glory, the next morning God restored my menstruation after six long years! Praise the Lord God of the Oracle!" Sister K. NJ

Our text-verse says "....he that believeth shall not make haste." Do you believe in the power of prophecy? Do not make haste just pray the following prayer in faith then wait on God!

Prayer: Lord I believe in You; I will wait on You for my testimony!

WORD SWORD OF THE ORACLE

The Word Today: Genesis 1:1 (NKJV)

*"In the beginning God created the **heavens** and the earth."*

HEAVEN [HEBREW] *SHAMAYIM*

The Hebrew word for heaven is *[Shamayim]* as used in Genesis 1:1, Genesis 1:8-9, Genesis 2:1, and Psalm 2:4 Strong concordance reference #8064. In Hebrew, the term heaven may refer to the physical atmosphere or the sky immediately above the earth, Genesis 2:1, Genesis 2:4, Genesis 2:19 i.e. the first heaven. The word heaven in the Hebrew refers also to the dwelling place of the Almighty God, the spiritual heaven or the third heavens. Psalm 14:2. This expression is derived from the word *"To be High and Lofty"* describing the Almighty God as being physically exalted, living in the heavens, above all other creatures. And even the physical heaven testifies to this; to God's glorious position and creative intelligence. Psalm 19:1 and Psalm 19:6. Heaven is the destination for believers. It is not physical but spiritual, being in the very presence of God. God is a Spirit Being that is impossible for human eyes to see. Heaven also is outside the boundaries and understanding of man as he lives in the physical universe. **Here are some Bible verses about Heaven and how to get there and what it's like.**

Matthew 5:17-20, Matthew 7:13-15, Matthew 19:16-19, Luke 13:29-33, John 14:2-4, Colossians 3:1-7, Revelation 7:13-17, Revelation 21:4-8, Revelation 22:3-9, Ezekiel 28:24-26, Matthew 22:29-33

Prayer: *Grant me the grace to make it to heaven in Jesus' name!*

CHURCH AND HOME SUNDAY SCHOOL

HOW DOES INIQUITY DIFFER FROM ORIGINAL SIN?

*A*s we discussed in our last study: while iniquity is weakness in us in a particular area of our life, because of sin and the sinful nature of our forefathers in us. Original sin is the total corruption of our nature because of our hostility against God that is in us as the result of the sin of Adam. *"So I said: "Woe is me, for I am undone! Because I am a man of unclean lips, and I dwell in the midst of a people of unclean lips; for my eyes have seen the King, the Lord of hosts."* Isaiah 6:5 [NKJV]

"For I do not understand my own actions [I am baffled, bewildered]. I do not practice or accomplish what I wish, but I do the very thing that I loathe [which my moral instinct condemns]. Now if I do [habitually] what is contrary to my desire, [that means that] I acknowledge and agree that the Law is good (morally excellent) and that I take sides with it. However, it is no longer I who do the deed, but the sin [principle] which is at home in me and has possession of me." Romans 7:15-17 [AMP]

CAN WE BE DELIVERED FROM THE CURSE OF INIQUITY?

Yes! Through faith in our Lord and Savior Jesus Christ; Who gave His body to be bruised at the Cross to deliver us from the curse of iniquity. Salvation is one of the divine benefits He bought for us.

"Who forgives all your iniquities, who heal all your diseases." Psalm 103:3 [NKJV]

"Blessed is the one whose sin the Lord does not count against them and in whose spirit is no deceit." Psalm 32:2 [NKJV] *"Speak tenderly to the heart of Jerusalem, and cry to her that her time of service and her warfare are ended, that [her punishment is accepted and] her iniquity is pardoned, that she has received [punishment] from the Lord's hand double for all her sins."* Isaiah 40:2 [AMP]

HOW CAN WE BE DELIVERED FROM THE CURSE OF INIQUITY?

Iniquity is purged when we recognize our inherent sins as such, acknowledge it, confess it, repent of it and ask God for mercy.

"Therefore I will judge you, O house of Israel, every one according to his ways," says the Lord God. *"Repent, and turn from all your transgressions, so that iniquity will not be your ruin."* Ezekiel 18:30 [NKJV] *[See also* 2 Timothy 2:25-26 [AMP]]

QUESTIONS:

Q1. HOW INIQUITY DOES DIFFERS FROM ORIGINAL SIN? Q2. CAN WE BE DELIVERED FROM THE CURSE OF INIQUITY? Q3. HOW CAN WE BE DELIVERED FROM THE CURSE OF INIQUITY?

> **Memory Verse:** "Blessed is the one whose sin the Lord does not count against them and in whose spirit is no deceit."
> Psalm 32:2 [NKJV]

Prayers:

1. Lord! Deliver me from all my iniquities in Jesus name!
2. Take not your Holy Spirit from me in Jesus name!
3. Thank You Lord for washing me in the blood of Jesus!

The Word Today: John 15:1-6

I DECLARE! I SHALL ALWAYS BE IN GOD'S PRESENCE!

The worse thing that can ever happen to a person is to be cast away from God's presence. In the passage above, Jesus used the relationship between a tree trunk and its branches to illustrate His relationship with us. According to Jesus, just like a branch that is cut from the trunk of a tree withers away with time, so also anyone who is not in Christ, who is separated from God, gradually but surely progresses to his/her destruction. Once God abandons you, you lose peace, direction, and boldness. Can you imagine King Saul who banished the practice of witchcraft in the land of Israel began to consult witches when God abandoned him? 1 Samuel 15 and 1 Samuel 28: Judas is another classic example of one who was cast away from God's presence. For three and a half years, Judas followed Jesus Christ as a disciple. He saw all the miracles, signs and wonders our Lord did, Judas was one of the twelve and seventy disciples sent out and he even cast out demons. Yet, because of love of money, he lost his place in eternal glory. I may not know who you are or what you do, but I pray that you shall not be cast out from the presence of the Lord in Jesus gracious' name. Amen!

Whatever you do, and in whatever situation you find yourself make sure you always remain in the presence of God. If you are presently not connected to God, you can do so by first surrendering your life to Jesus and then maintain your contact with Him through continual fellowship and obedience to His words. As you do so, you are blessed in Jesus' name. Amen!

Prayer: *Lord! Give me the grace to abide in Your presence!*

The Word Today: 1 Samuel 17:45-47

"Thou comest to me with a sword, and with a spear, and with a shield......"

I PROPHESY! ALL MY OBSTACLES SHALL BECOME MIRACLES!

The encounter of David with Goliath, the giant of Gath, was a giant opportunity disguised as a giant problem. At first, you would think and say what a huge problem, but it became a giant opportunity! Because David called on the name of the Lord and faced his obstacle head-on and he became victorious. I prophesy as you confront your hindrance in the name of the Lord you will have the same result as David in Jesus' name!

I don't know what trial and tribulation you may be facing right now, I don't know who the strange men or strange women are that are hindering you. I don't know the Goliath, the strongman or woman in your family, perpetuating household wickedness in your life or who that spirit of Goliath is; who is disguising as a supervisor, a manager or 'DAMAGER', which are workplace wickedness in your Job, your business, carrier or wherever. Today I decree the obstacles in your life shall all become miracles in the name of Jesus. Amen!

I'm praying for you, in the name of the Lord of Host even before the end of this month; your giant opportunities will show up in the name of Jesus. Amen! When David saw Goliath he just knew, he can't possibly miss a head that big. Opportunities so big that you cannot miss will come your way henceforth in Jesus' mighty name. Amen!

Prayer: O God of David fight for me today; turn all my obstacles to great opportunities for miracles, in Jesus' name. Amen!

The Word Today: Matthew 12:9-13

I PROPHESY! HENCEFORTH! NO ONE CAN STOP MY MIRACLE!

*I*f not for the fact that Jesus was determined to heal the man with the withered hand, the Pharisees would have stopped the man's miracle in its track with their legality. As far as they are concerned, it was against the law for Jesus to heal him on the Sabbath day. Since they were backed by law, they had legal grounds to stop that miracle. But fortunately for that man, Jesus was ready to by-pass legality to bless him that day. So also Jesus Christ is willing to do the same for you today. Many peoples' miracles are denied them in the spirit realm because of spiritual legalities in the same way as the man in our passage above. Most times God desires to release miracles to you but spiritual debates are raised up against your heart's desire by foundational and opposing powers to block your testimonies. Resulting in unanswered prayers; but when there is a divine intervention like in the case of the passage above, such situations are resolved in your favor. Have your testimonies been delayed or denied because of such legal grounds? Have you been waiting endlessly and in vain for a miracle all your life? Right now, I negate every spiritual argument working against you. By the power in the blood of Jesus, every legal ground empowering the enemy against you is hereby null and void in the mighty name of Jesus. I declare nobody can henceforth stop or hinder your miracles. For God is on your side so you will no more lack testimonies in Jesus' name. Amen!

Prayer: *Every legal ground against me is hereby nullified in Jesus' name. Amen*

The Word Today: Acts 12:5-7

"Peter was therefore kept in prison, but constant prayer was offered to God for him by the church.... bound with two chains between two soldiers; and the guards before the door were keeping the prison. Now behold, an angel of the Lord stood by him, and a light shone in the prison; and he struck Peter on the side and raised him up, saying, "Arise quickly!" And his chains fell off his hands."

EVERY SPIRITUAL CHAIN IN MY LIFE IS BROKEN NOW!

Indeed there is nothing prayer cannot do. Absolutely nothing! Apostle Peter was held bound in a fortress. With soldiers on guard to ensure that he did not escape. Peter was even chained to some of the soldiers inside the cell to ensure that their security arrangement was water-tight and full-proof. As far as King Herod was concerned, Peter's life was a done deal; the end of the road has finally come for Peter. But they did not know that the God that Peter served is able to do the impossible; He is able to open all doors without keys, even the doors of maximum security prisons. They forget He is the original door, the way, the truth and the life.

And when the prayers of the Saints reached heaven, God sent His angels of deliverance to set Peter free from captivity! You may be in one captivity or the other now! Maybe you are in a financial captivity. Or you have some household and/ or work place wickedness of the wicked fighting you. They may have held you and your loved ones bound for years. People may have vowed to devour your endeavors? I decree! The Lord shall send His angels of deliverance to set you free in Jesus' name. Amen!

Prayer: *Father! Send Your angels to set me free from captivity!*

The Word Today: 1 Samuel 27:1-7

"And it was told Saul that David had fled to Gath; so he sought him no more. Then David said to Achish, "If I have now found favor in your eyes, let them give me a place in some town in the country that I may dwell there. For why should your servant dwell in the royal city with you?" So Achish gave him Ziklag that day. Therefore Ziklag has belonged to the kings of Judah to this day."

I PROPHESY! MY ENEMIES SHALL FAVOR ME!

The Lord our God cannot be completely understood. No one can lay claim that he or she fully comprehend the Almighty God. This is because He sometimes does things that are completely unpredictable and unbelievable. Who would have thought that Achish, king of Gath could give a portion of land to David who brought disgrace and destruction to his people when he killed Goliath at the valley of Elah in 1 Samuel 17.

One would have thought that with the historic defeat of Goliath at the hands of David, the Philistine in general and the people of Gath in particular would have been sworn life-time enemies of David. But strange as it was, the people of Gath accommodated and even ceded a portion of their land to the same man who killed their kinsmen. Surely the anointing of favor upon David was at work. Today I transfer that same anointing upon you in the name of Jesus. Amen! Are you surrounded by enemies who desire your demise? Do your colleagues and peers seek your downfall? This day by the auction of the Spirit of the Lord God, I reverse that trend. Henceforth your enemies will favor you!

Prayer: *I receive the anointing of favor upon me; henceforth people will always favor me in Jesus' name. Amen!*

26

July 19th

WORD SWORD OF THE ORACLE

The Word Today: Genesis 5:24 (NKJV)

---

*"And Enoch **walked** with God; and he was not, for God took him."*

WALK [HEBREW] *HALAK*

[Halak] as used in Genesis 5:24, Genesis 6:9, Deuteronomy 13:4, Psalm 128:1, Micah 6:8 basically mean "to walk" [Strong's #1980.] *Halak* means "to walk", "to go", or "to travel." This word is most often used in the Old Testament to signify motion but also to connote habitual mannerism of life, of constant relationship and fellowship, with God Almighty. Genesis 13:17, 2 Samuel 11:2. And in this sense this word is used to describe God's relationship with faithful men like Noah, Enoch, Abraham and others in obedience to His commands. All through the Holy Scriptures, believers are called to walk with God daily, abiding in Him completely and trusting in Him entirely. 1 John 2:6, Galatians 5:16. Here are some other Bible verses about Walking with God. 2 Corinthians 5:7, Ephesians 2:10, Deuteronomy 5:33, Proverbs 3:5-6, James 4:7, 1 John 4:8, Romans 10:17, Psalms 119:105, 2 Corinthians 6:14, Romans 13:13, 2 Corinthians 5:17, 1 Corinthians 10:31, 1 Corinthians 1:9, Psalms 119:127, Psalms 37:1-40, Hebrews 11:5, 2 Timothy 3:16, John 4:24, John 1:14, Mark 2:13, Matthew 28:20, Matthew 28:19, Judges 4:7, Exodus 33:20, Genesis 5:1-32, Hebrews 11:1-40, 1 Thessalonians 5:17, Ephesians 5:18,   Ephesians 5:3, 2 Corinthians 5:21,   1 Corinthians 10:12, Acts 2:38, John 1:1, Mark 1:35, Amos 3:3, Isaiah 1:1-31, Job 22:21, 1 Kings 11:9, Joshua 1:8, John 3:16, Micah 6:8.

Prayer: *Lord! Grant me the grace to walk faithfully with You!*

CHURCH AND HOME SUNDAY SCHOOL

WHAT ASSURANCE DO WE HAVE THAT OUR INIQUITY WILL BE TAKEN AWAY?

Deliverance from iniquity is a part of the atonement which Jesus Christ procured for us at Calvary. If we ask for deliverance from iniquity and believe, He will grant it and deliverance is ours.

"If you ask anything in My name, I will do it. John 14:14 [NKJV]

"If we [freely] admit that we have sinned and confessed our sins, He is faithful and just (true to His own nature and promises) and will forgive our sins [dismiss our lawlessness] and [continuously] cleanse us from all unrighteousness [everything not in conformity to His will in purpose, thought, and action]." 1 John 1:9 [AMP]

"He shall see [the fruit] of the travail of His soul and be satisfied; by His knowledge of Himself [which He possesses and imparts to others] shall My [uncompromisingly] righteous One, My Servant, justify many and make many righteous (upright and in right standing with God), for He shall bear their iniquities and their guilt [with the consequences, says the Lord]. Isaiah 53:11 [AMP]

WILL OUR INIQUITIES BE VISITED ON OUR CHILDREN AFTER WE ARE DELIVERED FROM THEM?

No. When God pardons our iniquities, He casts them into the depths of the sea never to be remembered against us or our seeds.

"Who is a God like You, Pardoning iniquity and passing over the transgression of the remnant of His heritage? He does not retain His anger forever, because He delights in mercy. He will again have compassion on us, and will subdue our iniquities. You will cast all our sins into the depths of the sea." Micah 7:18-19 [NKJV]

"In those days and at that time, says the Lord, the iniquity of Israel will be sought, but there will be none, and the sins of Judah [will be sought], but none will be found, for I will pardon those whom I cause to remain as a remnant (the preserved ones who come forth after a long tribulation). Jeremiah 50:20 [AMP]

"You shall not bow down to them nor serve them. For I, the Lord your God, am a jealous God, visiting the iniquity of the fathers upon the children to the third and fourth generations of those who hate Me, but showing mercy to thousands, to those who love Me and keep My commandments." Exodus 20:5-6 [NKJV]

IS ANY MAN CAPABLE OF PERFECTLY KEEPING THE COMMANDMENT?

Yes. Christians can keep the commandment by walking in the spirit. Without the aid of the Holy Spirit natural man is not capable of keeping the commandments perfectly.

"For we have all become like one who is unclean [ceremonially, like a leper], and all our righteousness (our best deeds of rightness and justice) is like filthy rags or a polluted garment; we all fade like a leaf, and our iniquities, like the wind, take us away [far from God's favor, hurrying us toward destruction]. Isaiah 64:6 [AMP]

"Surely there is not a righteous man upon earth who does good and never sins." Ecclesiastes 7:20 [AMP]

"For God has done what the Law could not do, [its power] being weakened by the flesh, the entire nature of man without the Holy Spirit]. Sending His own Son in the guise of sinful flesh and as an offering for sin, [God] condemned sin in the flesh subdued, overcame, deprived it of its power over all who accept that sacrifice], So that the righteous and just requirement of the Law might be fully met in us who live and move not in the ways of the flesh but in the ways of the Spirit [our lives governed not by the standards and

according to the dictates of the flesh, but controlled by the Holy Spirit]. "Romans 8:3-4 [AMP]

"They have all turned aside, they have together become corrupt; there is none who does good, No, not one." Psalm 14:3.

SUNDAY SCHOOL QUESTIONS

Q1. WHAT ASSURANCE DO WE HAVE THAT OUR INIQUITY WILL BE TAKEN AWAY?
Q2. WILL OUR INIQUITY BE VISIT ON OUR CHILDREN AFTER WE ARE DELIVERED FROM THEM?
Q3. IS ANY MAN CAPABLE OF PERFECTLY KEEPING THE COMMANDMENT?

Memory Verse: "They have all turned aside, they have together become corrupt; there is none who does good, No, not one." Psalm 14:3 [NKJV]

Prayers:

I HAVE SINNED AGAINST YOU, AGAINST YOUR SON AND AGAINST THE HOLY GHOST HAVE MERCY ON ME!

I HAVE DONE SHADY DEALS AND BUSINESSES LORD HAVE MERCY ON ME IN JESUS' NAME.

July 21st

The Word Today: Genesis 39:2-4

"And the LORD was with Joseph, and he was a prosperous man; and he was in the house of his master the Egyptian....."

THE LORD SHALL PROSPER ME IN ALL MY ADVERSITIES!

In Genesis 39 Joseph's enemies would have succeeded in obliterating his dreams and glorious destiny if he had not secured God's abiding presence. In a series of negative progression, he lost his coat of many colors and his freedom. He was cast into a dry pit and eventually sold into slavery all in one day. I bet he never envisaged all this would happen to him when he woke up that fateful day.

Does this story relate to you one way or the other? Are your siblings trying to flush you and your dreams down the drain, is household and workplace wickedness bombarding you with one problem or the other? Listen to the Word of God, what the enemy meant for evil will turn out for good for you in Jesus' name. Amen! But despite his awful situation, Joseph experienced supernatural prosperity; he enjoyed both divine favor and promotion. I speak prophetically into your life now; the God of Joseph will cause you to experience supernatural prosperity, divine favor and promotion in all aspects of your life in Jesus' name. Amen! Joseph also enjoyed divine protection which kept him from death and destruction at the hands of "more powerful" people within and without. I prophesy... you will enjoy divine protection in the midst of powerful adversaries in Jesus' name. Amen!

Prayer: O God of Joseph cause me to experience supernatural prosperity all through my adversities in Jesus' name. Amen

31

The Word Today: 2 Samuel 5:1-3

I PROPHESY! MY RIVALS SHALL JOIN FORCES WITH ME!

*I*ndeed, in spite of the thoughts of men, only the counsel of God prevails in the lives of His saints. David's life proved that much. Before the passages above, David's claim to the throne was burdened with opposition. When Saul pursued him with the strength of the armed force of the nation of Israel, it seemed there was no hope of escape for David. When he eventually escaped into exile, it appeared that the kingship would forever remain elusive to him. The little ray of hope that shone at the death of King Saul was dimmed and dashed by Saul's loyalist, who immediately crowned Ishbosheth king over Israel:- 2 Samuel 2:8-10. But when the right time came, God arranged the circumstances perfectly well that all the tribes of Israel, including the family of late King Saul supported David's enthronement. Glory Alleluia to God!

Who are those gathered against your God ordained testimonies? Are there generational enemies that have fought against you for a long time now? Are your colleagues against your success in your career? Saint! Fear no more because the God of David is with you. The only thing you have to do is to ensure that you do His bidding and wrong no one willfully. As you do so, the same God who fought for David will fight your battles for you in Jesus' name. Amen! He shall cause your rivals and opponents to work together for your good in the mighty name of Jesus. Amen!

Prayers: *Lord Jesus! Command my entire opponent to join force with me in the name of Jesus Christ. Amen!*

The Word Today: Deuteronomy 8:18

I PROPHESY! MY MIRACLE SHALL BE INSTANTLY AWESOME!

*A*brother just got a breakthrough job. He says it is beyond his wildest dreams. Before that could happen though, there were certain prayers he had been praying ever since he connected with this ministry at the beginning of this year. Hear his testimony:

"I got to know about your ministry when a friend sent me a copy of your book "the oracle of God prophetic devotional" I joined and always partook of the monthly 3 days fasting and praying: that occurs at the 1ˢᵗ 2ⁿᵈ and 3ʳᵈ of every month since I connected earlier this year. And I've been believing God that this is my year of breakthrough that will shock my enemies and surprise my loved ones. Early last month before I attended a job interview I emailed Rev. Stevie and he sent me some prayer points which I prayed fervently and God gave me a job which is far beyond my wildest dreams. These are the prayers that the Oracle of God sent to me that I prayed: Brethren join me in thanking God who is able to do exceedingly above what we pray, ask for or think. Praise the LORD. Brother JKL

1. *I paralyze every power of failure at the edge of my breakthrough in the name of Jesus. Amen!*
2. *You gates of employment opportunity, whatever is holding you from manifesting in my life, by the unchallengeable power of God, crash and open now!*
3. *Let divine harvest fall upon me and fill my life by fire!*
4. *O God let the Power of the anointing to get great job fall upon me now in Jesus' mighty name. Amen!*

5. *O Lord my Father, speak mercy and favor to my job situation in Jesus' name. Amen!*

6. *O Lord my God roll-away every barrier to my ordained job in Jesus' name. Amen!*

7. *O Lord in Heaven, I plead the Blood of Jesus upon my job situation and I ask for favor to come upon me during the interview in the Name of Jesus. Amen!*

8. *I reject the spirit of the tail in my employment and I claim the spirit of the head in the Name of Jesus. Amen!*

9. *I receive the power to overcome and to excel among all the job competitors in the Name of Jesus. Amen!*

10. *Holy Spirit, have your way in me, in Jesus name. Amen!*

11. *This month and all the days of my life: I stand against every falsehood in me, in the name of Jesus. Amen!*

12. *My Father, do a new thing in my life that will put my enemies to perpetual shame in Jesus' name. Amen!*

13. *My father, manifest your power in my life this month.*

14. *My Lord and My God let my lines fall unto pleasant places this month in the name of Jesus. Amen! Psalm 16:6.*

15. *Bondage of darkness over my life, break now by fire!*

16. *Any evil gathering summoned for my destruction, and distraction be scattered unto desolation in Jesus' name!*

17. *Evil force against my life and my handiwork, scatter by fire in the name of Jesus. Amen!*

18. *Wicked powers, anywhere challenging the power of God in me, scatter unto desolation, in Jesus name!*

19. *Every habitation of wickedness in my life, scatter by fire!*

20. *Every yoke of failure upon my life, break by fire.*

21. *Every yoke of poverty upon my life, break by fire!*

22. *Thank You Lord Jesus for answering my prayers in the name of Jesus. Amen!*

THE WORD TODAY: Lamentation 3:22-23 [AMP]

"It is because of the Lord's mercy and loving-kindness that we are not consumed, because His [tender] compassions fail not. They are new every morning; great and abundant is Your stability and faithfulness."

I PROPHESY! I WILL NOT BE CONSUMMED BY EVIL!

*M*any are unaware of the mercies of God in their lives. And those who are aware are not appreciative of it. They make plans without recourse to God. Some speak as though they regulate their existence. Such was the folly of King Nebuchadnezzar of Babylon in Daniel 4. I don't know what your disposition toward God is, but I do know that it is not by your power that you are alive today. After all; there are many people who are smarter, wiser, wealthier, and holier than you who are dead. So, the fact that you are alive is not because you are better than those who have died, but for the goodness and mercies of God upon you.

So, instead of agonizing over the things that God is yet to do for you, you should rather appreciate whatever He has already done for you. If you can reflect on the good things that the good LORD has done so far for you; even without you asking Him to, He will do more for you. You will be able to appreciate Him even more; if you take a visit to the emergency room [ER] and the ICU wards of hospitals you will really have cause to glorify God for His mercies and goodness in your life. Now if you really understand what I am saying right here; can you just lift up your hands and your voice and just bless the name of the Lord before you pray the following prayer?

Prayer: *By the blood of Jesus I shall not be consumed by evil!*

July 25th

THE WORD TODAY: 1 John 3:8 [NIV]

"....The reason the Son of God appeared was to destroy the devil's work."

EVERY EVILL PATTERN IN MY LIFE IS DESTROYED!

"Prior to my joining the Maryland campus of the Oracle of God Int'l Ministries, there was nothing to say about my life. Sin had dominion over me; I was addicted to sin. I am always having one sickness or the other to struggle with. I am always on one kind prescription drug or more, consuming them two to three times every day. My eating habit was terrible, lack of appetite, but always drinking alcoholic beverages. I know my life was not in order, but I simply could not help myself. One day, I obeyed an altar call and gave my life to Jesus Christ. Soon after, I noticed a drastic change in my life. First, I noticed that my health began to improve as those incessant illnesses just disappeared one after the other. With time, I observed that the urge to sin no longer had a hold on me. Today by the grace of God all those evil patterns in my life are all gone. I now live a clean and wonderful life as a Christian. I give all the glory to God the Father, the Son Jesus Christ and the Holy Spirit." Brother I. MD

What has the enemy used to bind you? Is it sin and sickness? Is it addiction to controlled substance? Is there an evil pattern in your life? Is there a reproach you are dealing with? Is it a habit that you are unable to break free from? Place them at the feet of our Lord and savior Jesus Christ now! He is the only power that can destroy every yoke in your life. 1 John 3:8 says it is for that reason He came to the world. Allow Him to take control and things will change for good for you in Jesus' name. Amen!

Prayer: Every evil pattern in my life is destroyed in Jesus' name!

36

July 26ᵗʰ

WORD SWORD OF THE ORACLE

The Word Today: Genesis 1:10 (NKJV)

*"And God called the dry **land** Earth, and the gathering together of the waters He called Seas. And God saw that it was good."*

LAND [HEBREW] *'ERETS*

A Strong's concordance #776 recorded the use of land in Genesis 1:1, Genesis 1:10, Genesis 4:16, Genesis 13:13, Deuteronomy 34:2 and Psalm 98:3 and the usual Old Testament use of the word Land is *Erets* in the Hebrew language. This word has several meaning, including earth in contrast to Sea Genesis 1:10 and in contrast to heaven Genesis 1:1. Land is also used in the sense of ground as plot of real estate or as a geographical location. Genesis 4:16. It also extends to land as of a sovereign nation Genesis 13:10, Genesis 13:12. Land also refers to even people who live upon the earth as in Psalm 98:3, Psalm 100:1. In essence, all land belongs to God the creator of all things. Psalm 24:1. So when God promised the People of Israel the "Land" of Canaan, it was His to give. Because the land of Canaan was a very important element in God's covenant with the Children of Israel, the descendants of Abraham Genesis 12:1-3, Genesis 13:15, Genesis 15:7.

Here are some other Bible verses about Land: Ps. 2:8, Rev. 16:13, Matt. 5:42, Prov. 27:23, Prov. 12:10, 1 Sam. 17:34, 1 Tim. 1:8-10, 2 Thess. 2:9, Rom. 13:4, Luke 12:33, Matt. 10:29, Matt. 6:26, Micah 5:12, Eze. 13:18-20, Jer. 27:9, Isa. 25:4, Prov. 6:6-8, Ps. 127:1-14, Ps. 104:5, Job 38:41, Job 12:7-10, Deut. 25:4, Deut. 22:4-7, Deut. 18:9-12, Deut. 17:2-5, Deut. 4:19, Leviticus 25:7, Leviticus 20:13, Leviticus 18:22 Exodus 23:11, Exodus 23:5 Exodus 20:10, Genesis 1:1-31 and Jude 1:7.

37

4th Sunday of the Month of July

CHURCH AND HOME SUNDAY SCHOOL

CAN WE ALL BE SAVED BY KEEPING THE COMMANDMENTS?

No! Man cannot be saved just by keeping the commandments.

"Now it is evident that no person is justified (declared righteous and brought into right standing with God) through the Law, for the Scripture says, The man in right standing with God [the just, the righteous] shall live by and out of faith and he who through and by faith is declared righteous and in right standing with God shall live.
Galatians 3:11 [AMP]

WHAT THEN IS THE PURPOSE OF THE TEN COMMANDMENTS?

The law or the Ten Commandments have threefold purpose: *"For no person will be justified (made righteous, acquitted, and judged acceptable) in His sight by observing the works prescribed by the Law. For [the real function of] the Law is to make men recognize and be conscious of sin [not mere perception, but an acquaintance with sin which works toward repentance, faith, and holy character].* Romans 3:20 [AMP]

1. They act as a curb by checking, to some extent, the outbursts of sin in the world.
2. They act as a mirror by showing us our sins.
3. They act as rules to teach us which works are pleasing to God.

"Knowing and understanding this: that the Law is not enacted for the righteous (the upright and just, who are in right standing with God), but for the lawless and unruly, for the ungodly and sinful, for the irreverent and profane, for those who strike and beat and [even]

murder fathers and strike and beat and [even] murder mothers, for manslayers." 1Timothy 1:9 [AMP]

NOTE: The Ten Commandments were written on two tablets of stone. The first table of Law deals with man's relationship to God. While the second one deal with man's relationship to his fellowman.

"And He replied to him, You shall love the Lord your God with all your heart and with all your soul and with all your mind (intellect). This is the greatest (most important, principal) and first commandment. And a second is like it: You shall love your neighbor as [you do] yourself." Matthew 22:37-38 [AMP]

SUNDAY SCHOOL QUESTIONS

Q1. CAN WE ALL BE SAVED BY KEEPING THE COMMANDMENTS? Q2. WHAT THEN IS THE PURPOSE OF THE TEN COMMANDMENTS? Q3. HOW MANY TABLETS WAS THE TEN COMMANDMENTS WRITTEN ON? Q4. HOW DO THEY DIFFER?

Memory Verse: Psalm 119:9 *"How can a young man cleanse his way? By taking heed according to Your word."*

Today's Prayers

1. *My life shall not prosper in sin in the name of Jesus.*

2. *Lord! Let Your Word cleanse me now in Jesus' name.*

3. *O God! Help me live a righteous life in Jesus' name!*

4. *Thank You Lord for Your Mercy in Jesus' name!*

MY GOD SHALL SET MY ENEMIES AGAINST EACH OTHER!

*D*ue to their historical opposition and resistance to the freedom of the Israelites in Exodus chapters 7-14, the Egyptians incurred the wrath of God and thus became His enemy. Consequently, over time, the land of Egypt began to symbolize the land of captivity and opposition to God and His people. So many times, when God refers to Egypt and the Egyptians in the scriptures, He often times, simply means enemies of His Children. So, today Biblical references to the land of Egypt go beyond the geographical region called Egypt in North Africa to represent every enemy of God's people; by implication, anyone who stands in opposition to you, an upright born again Believer can be appropriately described as an Egyptian.

So, the reference to Egyptians in our passage above is actually talking about your enemies. According to the passage, the Lord has declared that He will set them against each other. The implication is that, instead of coming together in agreement against you, they will begin to disagree with and against each other. Their disagreement will lead to conflicts in their camp which will culminate in their destruction. Are there Egyptians in your life that has refused to allow you peace of mind? Arise now and begin to command them to fight against each other. As you do so, the Lord of Host shall set all your enemies against each other in the name of Jesus. Just prepare to enjoy the spoils of their war. Prepare to celebrate your testimonies in Jesus' name!

Prayer: *I command every Egyptian in my life to begin to fight it out among themselves in the name of Jesus. Amen!*

"In that day,' says the Lord of hosts, 'the peg that is fastened in the secure place will be removed and be cut down and fall, and the burden that was on it will be cut off; for the Lord has spoken."

EVERY GENERATIONAL CURSE IN MY BLOOD LINE IS BROKEN!

A sure place is a phrase that simply means a secure and firm position. When a nail is fastened to a sure place, it becomes secure and difficult to remove. A typical example is a nail that is fixed firmly into a wall. Except a very strong force is applied on the wall, such a nail cannot be easily removed. So, when the scripture refers to a nail that is fastened in the sure place, it refers to age-old or generational problems which cannot be wished away or removed by minor attempts. Such problems can only be resolved when the power of God descends on them. That is exactly what our text-verse above is saying to us today. I do not know what problem has remained unresolved in your family lineage for a long time now. Is it a curse of untimely death? Is it acidic poverty? Is it that people from your particular city, town or village cannot aspire beyond and above certain level of achievement? Is the curse in your lineage that of wrong spouse? Is it bareness? There is good news for you this day! There is solution for you and the solution is that as soon as the mouth of the LORD speaks it, the age-long curses or bondage is destroyed in the name of Jesus. Amen! This day, as the mouthpiece of Jehovah God, I decree concerning you; every generational curse in your blood line is broken in Jesus' name!

Prayer:

I invoke the anointing of the Spirit of God to destroy every generational curse in my life in Jesus' name. Amen!

The Word Today: Luke 6:28 [KJV]

"Bless them that curse you, and pray for them which despitefully use you."

I RECEIVE THE GRACE TO PRAY WITH GREAT RESULTS!

We all know we need a successful prayer life. But very few, especially Believers ever have a successful prayer life. The main reason why many Saints struggle with prayer is because of all the wrong teachings they have had. We have been misled to believe that prayer is to try to sway God to manifest His power concerning our needs. We believe we can save, heal, and deliver by swaying God; as if He is waiting on us to shape up and earn it.

The truth is, we cannot and don't even deserve it, and will never be good enough when we cannot even pray for our enemies. But because of Jesus, the entirety of God's possession becomes ours by grace through faith in Him. That's good news right there. So you no longer need to beg; but just exercise by faith, the delegated authority Jesus Christ has given unto you and then receive His blessings upon your life. Your long list of unanswered prayer is also a result of your unbelief.

PRAY THE WORD OF GOD NOW!

Psalm 34:10 says *"the young lions do suffer lack, and hunger: but they that seek the Lord shall not lack any good thing."* Lord, I seek You this day, from now on I will not lack any good thing in Jesus name. Amen!

John 3:16 says *"for God so love the world that he gave his begotten son that whosoever believeth in Him shall not perish but have everlasting life."* Father, I have heard of your great love, please, extend it to me today in Jesus name. Amen!

I AM DELIVERED FROM THE PHILISTINES OF MY DESTINY!

$\mathscr{A}$t the death of Priest Eli, the Philistines defeated Israelites and took away the ark of covenant. With the presence of God amongst them gone, the children of Israel became miserable. Even the return of the ark in 1 Samuel 6 could not restore the confidence of Israel; but when the Oracle of God, Prophet Samuel, showed up in the scene with the anointing and with the knowledge of what is required to be done to revive Israel, everything changed for good; a revival broke out. Things are going to change for you this day in Jesus' name. Amen! Prophet Samuel admonished them to confess, repent, fast, and renounce the idols in their lives. The outcome was divine intervention. The LORD will divinely intervene in your situation this day in the name of Jesus. Amen! Are you one of such backslidden Believers? Have you gone back deep into the pigs' pen? If you have, then there is need for you to make a U-Turn, confess, repent and restitute your ways. There is still a chance for you to change; and that time is now. All you have to do is to pray thus: *Lord Jesus! I rededicate my life to you, forgive my sins [MENTION THEM] cleans me in your precious blood which you shed at Calvary. Have mercy upon me and please grant me salvation, grant me dominion and power over sin in Jesus' name.* As you pray this prayer, I prophesy, you are now a victor and never again a victim in Jesus' name. Amen!

Prayer: *Fear and failure, be bound and cast out of my life in the name of Jesus Christ; henceforth, I am moving forward and upward because I am a victor not a victim in Christ Jesus. Amen!*

43

The Word Today: Psalm 22:3

"But thou art holy, O thou that inhabitest the praises of Israel."

THE LORD GOD SHALL INHABIT MY PRAISE!

𝒫raise is one of God's principles that work wonders when applied. Praising God brings God to your rescue. Praising God without being forced to bring unspeakable joy. Psalm 16:11 says *"Thou wilt shew me the path of life: in thy presence is fullness of joy; at thy right hand there are pleasures for evermore".* You cannot be joyful if you are not "PRAISE -FULL" or full of praise! Be thankful therefore, praise God now and forever!

WORSHIP AND ADORE GOD NOW:

Lord, my heart is fixed within me! I will praise and magnify Your Holy Name all the days of my life! I will adore You like never before! It doesn't matter what is going on right now in my life, I will lift You higher on a daily basis! I will bless Your Holy Name! You are worthy to be praised and adored! You are worthy to be magnified! You are the Rock of Ages, the Bright and Morning Star, the conquering Lion of the tribe of Judah! Your praise shall continually be in my mouth in Jesus' name I worship. Amen!

AUGUST BIRTHDAY AND WEDDING ANNIVERSARY PRAYERS!

Father I thank You for Your children; born in the month of August and those commemorating their wedding this eighth month of the year. The month of restoration, the month of new beginnings; Father, in their lives, do something new, bless and prosper them anew; let them become more dedicated to you. Let it be well with them in Jesus' mighty name. Amen!

WORD SWORD OF THE ORACLE

The Word Today: Genesis 15:6 (NKJV)

---

*"And he **believed** in the Lord, and He accounted it to him for righteousness."*

BELIEVE [HEBREW] *AMAN*

The word believe i.e. *[Aman]* in the Hebrew language as used in our text-verse above and also in Exodus 4:31, 2 Chronicles 20:20, Psalm 11:10 [Strong's #539] has the root meaning 'to establish' or 'to confirm.' The English word Amen, which is used to express approval, comes from the same root word, Nehemiah 5:13, Psalm 41:13. Belief is one of the most important ideas in the Scripture, because a person must believe God through Jesus Christ His only begotten Son in order to be saved from the bondage and captivity of sin and iniquity. For this very reason, the New Testament makes much of the fact that Abraham believed God and it was accounted for righteousness Hebrews 11:8-12.

Whenever the scriptures, be it the Old Testament or the New Testament states that a person believes in the Lord God, it signals that the person has made a conscious decision to treat God's word as certain and has made a commitment to do what God wants and commands. Genesis 15:6, John 1:12.

Here are some Bible verses about Belief in the Bible: Matthew 21:22, Romans 15:13, John 3:16, Mark 5:36, Matthew 21:32, Psalms 78:32-33, Numbers 14:11, John 6:35, 1 John 4:16, Colossians 2:7, Ephesians 2:8-9, Matthew 9:28, Habakkuk 1:5, Isaiah 43:10, Psalms 106:24, Psalms 27:13, 2 Chronicles 20:20.

45

Prayer: *Lord Jesus! Forgive my unbelief in Jesus' name. Amen!*

1ˢᵗ Sunday of the Month of August

CHURCH AND HOME SUNDAY SCHOOL

THE FIRST TABLE OF THE LAW

WHAT IS THE FIRST COMMANDMENT?

"Thou shalt have no other gods before me". Exodus 20:3

WHAT ARE WE COMMANDED BY THIS FIRST COMMANDMENT?

We are commanded to offer God alone the supreme worship that is due Him.

"Then Jesus said to him, "Away with you,[a] Satan! For it is written, 'You shall worship the Lord your God, and Him only you shall serve." Matthew 4:10 [NKJV]

"I am the Lord, that is My name; And My glory I will not give to another, Nor My praise to carved images". Isaiah 42:8 [NKJV]

WHAT IS FORBIDDEN BY THE FIRST COMMANDMENT?

1. We are forbidden to set up any creature or object as the chief object of our worship, the chief source of our happiness, or chief teacher of truth. This is making a god out of something created.

"But our God is in heaven; He does whatever He pleases. Their idols are silver and gold, the work of men's hands".
Psalm 115:3-4 [NKJV]

BIBLE NARATIVE:

THE WORSHIP OF THE GOLDEN CALF BY THE ISRAELITES IN EXODUS 32

THE PEOPLE WORSHIPED BAAL IN 1 KINGS 18:18-29

THE PHILISTINE MADE DAGON THEIR GOD JUDGES 16:23-24

2. We are forbidden to believe in a god that is not the Triune God.

"That all should honor the Son just as they honor the Father. He who does not honor the Son does not honor the Father who sent Him." John 5:23 [NKJV]

3. We are forbidden to fear, love or trust, in any person or thing more than God. It is a sin to attribute to a creature or thing a power that belongs to God alone, such as using charms and spells, believing in fortune-tellers, or going to spiritualists.

"And do not fear those who kill the body but cannot kill the soul. But rather fear Him who is able to destroy both soul and body in hell." Matthew 10:28 [NKJV]

"He who loves [and takes more pleasure in] father or mother more than [in] Me is not worthy of Me; and he who loves [and takes more pleasure in] son or daughter more than [in] Me is not worthy of Me". Matthew 10:37 [AMP]

"Lean on, trust in, and be confident in the Lord with all your heart and mind and do not rely on your own insight or understanding." Proverbs 3:5 [AMP]

47

"They are doomed and their fate is eternal misery (perdition); their god is their stomach (their appetites, their sensuality) and

they glory in their shame, siding with earthly things and being of their party." Philippians 3:19 "(AMP)

BIBLE NARRATIVES:

THE RICH MAN AND POOR LAZARUS THE BEGGER:
LUKE 16:19-31 *[the rich man thought more of costly clothes and good food.]*

JESUS AND THE RICH MAN SEEKING THE KINGDOM
OF GOD: Matthew 19:16-22 *[the young rich ruler loved his possessions more than he love Jesus Christ.]*

SUNDAY SCHOOL QUESTIONS

Q1. WHAT IS THE FIRST COMMANDMENT? Q2. WHAT ARE WE COMMANDED BY THIS FIRST COMMANDMENT? Q3. WHAT IS FORBIDDEN BY THE FIRST COMMANDMENT?

Today's Memory Verse:
Exodus 20:3 *"Thou shalt have no other gods before me."*

Today's Prayers

1. No agenda of my life shall be higher than God in Jesus' name. 2. Every witchcraft animal assigned to rule me in my dream, die by fire in the name of Jesus.   3. Powers of darkness stealing and demanding worship from me in the dream, I stop your activities now and I command you to die by fire in Jesus' name!   4. I barricade my life with the fire of The Holy Ghost and the blood of Jesus from every idol in the name of Jesus. Amen!

48

The Word Today: Isaiah 43:18-19

I AM EMPOWERED BY GOD FOR A NEW BEGINNING!

The month of August is the month of a new beginning. Number eight is the number of rest or the restart number. So I prophesy the Lord God will start a new thing in your life this month in the name of Jesus! If you repent and decide to change your sinful ways and follow the counsel of God, you will experience a dramatic change in every area of your life in the name of Jesus. The end of your sinful, hopeless, weary and frustrating life marks the beginning of a new and vibrant life in Christ Jesus. No matter what you are going through now God can still, and will still make a way for you and your loved ones in Jesus' name.

Your case may be like a crying man, whose wife of twenty five years just passed. After spending all their savings battling cancer! Your situation may be like a couple who lost all their investment in a deal gone bad. And yet your condition may be like a brother who suddenly finds himself jobless after he just got married and his wife is now pregnant of twins. Yet again your circumstance could be like the sister who cried with unbelief when her fiancé called off their engagement because he found someone else. Your case may be like any of the above. Whatever the situation; the death of a loved one, business collapse, unemployment, singleness, bareness, divorce, broken promises and disappointment, just have faith in God! God is ever faithful and He will never deny Himself 2 Timothy 2:13. He will never leave you nor forsake you Hebrews 13:5. He will do a new thing for you this season in the name of Jesus. Amen!

Prayer: *O Lord! Do a new thing in my life in Jesus' name!*

The Word Today: Isaiah 43:1-5

I DECREE! I SHALL BE PRESERVED IN TIMES OF TROUBLE!

Almost every Believer, at one point in time, gets to a point of confusion when they begin to wonder whether they are still in right standing with God. Such are difficult times when those involved experience extreme afflictions, infirmities, difficulties travails etc. At such times, God requires of every Saint, an absolute trust in His ability to deliver. In our word today, God assured us that He is aware of such situations. In fact, He uses such circumstances to prove His might. That is what He did in the case of Shedrach, Meshach and Abednego in Daniel 3. He allowed them to be put in the fiery furnace before He proved Himself by ensuring that the fire which was at a very high temperature did not hurt them.

Are you going through a crisis period? God did not say you would not pass through crisis. He said that He would be there with you. If He is there with you, the crisis cannot consume you, no matter how difficult it seems. Saint, there is always a way out with God. Job lost everything he had: his children, houses, animals, wealth, his health etc. But as he held on to God, everything he lost was restored unto him seven folds. David was a fugitive for a long period. He lived in bushes, wilderness, and caves with vagabonds, snakes, scorpions for neighbors. He walked through the valley of the shadow of death for most of seventeen years. Yet, no harm came upon him because he trusted in God. Do you desire such victory? Just put your trust in God and He will see you through all your trials in Jesus' name.

Prayer: *Lord! Preserve me in times of tribulation in Jesus' name!*

The Word Today: 2 Kings 3:9-17

I DECREE! THIS IS MY SEASON OF DIVINE PROVISION!

God has several ways of proving His might in adverse situations. Thereby increasing the faith of those in difficulties; the situation in the above scripture is a case in point. Before the three Kings came to Elisha, they had wondered in the desert in search of direction. Consequently, their confidence had been battered. In fact they had concluded that God had decided to hand them over to the king of Moab. So they were discouraged, faithless, and hopeless. God knew that if they had to win the war, they needed to recover their confidence and faith. That is why He showed them that sign of divine provision. Had Elisha commanded it to rain, they would not have been too surprised. In fact, they may even believe that it was a coincidence.

But the manner in which God provided water to assuage their thirst was in a form that only He could do. Saint, are you discouraged and in despair because of the lack you have suffered recently. Have you come to the conclusion that God has forsaken you? Despair no more. You are still very important in God's scheme of things. He is still an expert in the process of supernatural provision. Today, as the Oracle of God, I prophesy that this is your season of divine provision. I tell you Saint, prophetic declarations are meant to lift the oppressed out of their adverse conditions. Those who get the best out of such declarations are people who believe and key into them. Do you agree with this prophecy? Then receive it now in Jesus' name!

Prayer: *I receive my supernatural provision as declared by the Oracle of God in Jesus' mighty name. Amen!*

I DECREE! MY DETRACTORS SHALL BOW TO ME!

The Spirit of God is going to come upon you this day and a new anointing will begin to operate in your life in the name of Jesus. Amen! And all your detractors will bow to you in Jesus' name. In 2 Kings 2:1-15 the other sons of the prophet mocked the diligence of Elisha. But when a double portion of the spirit of Elijah came upon Elisha, and as a result he smote River Jordan asunder he immediately gained the respect of all the other prophets in the nation.

Have you been mocked by scorners, have your Christian faith being ridiculed? Have you been discriminated against and humiliated for your faith in Christ Jesus? Hold on to the plough, for the anointing that breaks the yoke is coming upon you this day! I decree every jesters and mockers in your life, limiting your success shall be uprooted in Jesus' name. Amen!

In Mark 10:46-52 those who were telling Bartimeus to shut up, were the same people that Jesus sent to get him for his breakthrough, and when they saw the beggar with brand new eyes, they celebrated him. I prophesy unto you now, you will be celebrated where you have been rejected in the name of Jesus. I decree, those who are mocking you now will come and celebrate with you in Jesus' name. Amen!

Prayer: *Lord Jesus! Bring upon me a double portion of Your Spirit! By the power of the anointing that breaks yokes, I decree and declare every of my detractors must bow to me from henceforth in Jesus' name. Amen!*

The Word Today: Numbers 14:28

"Say unto them, as truly as I live, saith the LORD, as ye have spoken in mine ears, so will I do to you:"

I PROFESS MY CONFESSIONS OF THE WORD OF GOD!

Heavenly Father, I attend to Your Word. I incline my ears unto Your sayings. I refuse to let them depart from my eyes. I keep them in the midst of my heart, for they are life and health to all my flesh. Proverbs 5:1 says my son, attend unto my wisdom, and bow thine ear to my understanding:
Proverbs 10:27 says the fear of the Lord prolongeth days: but the years of the wicked shall be shortened.
Proverbs 13:3 says He that keepeth his mouth keepeth his life: but he that openeth wide his lips shall have destruction.

Lord Jesus! You have given me abundant life. I receive it through Your Word and that life flows to every organ and tissue of my body bringing life and health to me. John 10:10 says the thief cometh not, but to steal, to kill, and to destroy: I am come that they might have life, and that, they might have it more abundantly. John 6:63 says It is the spirit that quickeneth; the flesh profiteth nothing: the words that I speak unto you, they are spirit, and they are life. I am FREE from unforgiveness and strife. I forgive others as Christ has forgiven me, for the love of God is shed abroad in my heart by the Holy Ghost. Matthew 6:12 says and forgive us our debts, as we forgive our debtors. Romans 5:5 say and hope maketh not ashamed; because the love of God is shed abroad in our hearts by the Holy Ghost which is given unto us. In Jesus' name I PROFESS THIS CONFESSION!

WORD SWORD OF THE ORACLE

The Word Today: Genesis 15:6 (NKJV)

---

*"And he believed in the Lord, and He **accounted** it to him for righteousness."*

ACCOUNTED [HEBREW] *CHASCHAB*

In Strong's #2803 is the word *"accounted"* as used in our text-verse above and in Exodus 26:1, Isaiah 33:8. The word Hebrew word for accounted is *"Chaschab"* this is a very complex verb in the range of two very distinct meaning. The first is associated with calculations of some sort *"count"* Leviticus 25:27, Proverbs 17:28, *"esteem"* Isaiah 53:3, *"impute"* 2 Samuel 19:19, *"reckon"* Leviticus 27:18, Leviticus 27:23. The usage of the word *"Chaschab or account"* includes the element of planning. So the word also has the meaning of *"think"* 1 Samuel 1:13, *"devise"* Esther 8:3, *"artistic design"* Exodus 26:1, Exodus 35:35 or *"regard"* Isaiah 33:8. As also used in Genesis 15:6, the word also has commercial connotations. Abram's faith was *"accounted"* to him for righteousness, that is, computed or totaled as a credit or deposit in Abram's account or favor. Paul also appeals to this credit and debt language of the accounting ledger in his explanation of justification by faith in Romans 4:3.

Here are some Bible verse about "Accounted"

Deut. 2:11, Deut. 2:20, 1 Kings 10:21, 2 Chr. 9:20, Ps. 22:30, Isa. 2:22, Mark 10:42, Luke 20:35, Luke 21:36, Luke 22:24, Romans 8:36, Galatians 3:6.

Prayers

1. O Lord My God! Let my faith be accounted for righteousness!
2. Let my belief in You bring me to divine favor in Jesus' name!

CHURCH AND HOME SUNDAY SCHOOL

WHEN DO WE LOVE GOD ABOVE ALL THINGS?

We love God above all things when we gladly devote our lives to His service, firmly believe what God has revealed and then profess these beliefs openly whenever and wherever necessary. *"Jesus said to him, "You shall love the Lord your God with all your heart, with all your soul, and with all your mind."* Matthew 22:37

WHEN DO WE TRUST GOD ABOVE ALL THINGS?

We trust God above all things when we completely commit our lives to keeping His Laws; when we rely upon Him for help in our need, and believe in God's faithfulness to keep His promises no matter what.

"It is better to trust in the Lord. Than to put confidence in man." Psalm 118:8 [NKJV]

"Trust in the Lord with all your heart, and lean not on your own understanding;" Proverbs 3:5 [NKJV]

Questions: *q1. When do we love god above all things? q2. When do we trust god above all things? q3. What are benefits of trusting god?*

Memory Verse: "It is better to trust in the Lord; than to put confidence in man." Psalm 118:8 [NKJV]

Prayer: *Lord! Empower me to trust and serve You well in the name of Jesus. Amen!*

I DECREE! WHATSOEVER I DO I SHALL PROSPER IN IT!

*A*bove in the word today is the formula for prosperity at all times. If you apply the principles embedded therein, you will not fail in your endeavors. As long as you abide by the dictates of the Psalm above, you are sure to prosper. Many Believers are unable to benefit from this passage because of partial obedience. They avoid the counsel of the ungodly; they stay away from evil works and evil deeds but still complain of lack of desired result in life. The problem is that, most often than not, they do not meditate and delight in the word of God. They are too busy with the issues of life, that they do not spend quality time on the word of God except on Sundays; the only day they hear the word. If you are one of such people, the time has come for you to change. If you are too busy for God, then you are too busy for the manifestation of the supernatural in your life. But when you spend quality time with the scripture, and you are in obedience to divine directives, the supernatural will become very natural in your life. A man took time off from his busy schedule and abandoned an important appointment for a contract which he had pursued for a long time, to attend Bible study in one of our assemblies. As he left the Bible study he got an alert from his bank that his letter of credit running into hundreds of thousands of US Dollars has cleared. The money had been tied down for years after completing the job. When you get busy with the things of God, He will get busy with your business. Do you desire to prosper? Do 'The Word" and you shall prosper!

Prayer: *Father! Grant me the grace to fulfill Your counsel!*

I SHALL FULFILL THE REQUISTE FOR PROSPERITY!

*M*any Believers have committed to memory, prayed and recited the above passage constantly and diligently to no avail. They fail because they considered the passage in isolation. They have not considered and applied verse three [3] as a continuation of the sentence that started from verse one [1] of psalm chapter number one [1]. Such believers believed that God's desire for them is without conditions. Consequently, they err in their effort to appropriate God's blessings without fulfilling His conditions. And they are worse off for it, because it results in spiritual poverty, constant and continuous failure.

In our working scripture today, God made it clear that the prerequisite to enjoy the promises of prosperity, abundance, wealth and health etc., is to avoid the company of sinners, and sinful habits. Furthermore, He asserts in verse number two [2] that such a person should meditate in the word of God daily. Fulfillment; of the above conditions ensure a connection to God, who is the original source of all blessings and every other source is just a resource.

Do you desire to prosper in your endeavors? Then you need to develop a good relationship with God. As you do so, I prophesy the LORD God will enable you to fulfill the requisites to prosper and prosper you indeed in Jesus' gracious name. Amen!

Prayer: *Lord Jesus! I desire prosperity! Enable me to fulfill your conditions in the name of Jesus. Amen!*

www.oogod.org/ *pastor@oogod.org*

August 13th

The Word Today: Deuteronomy 29:29, Proverbs 25:2

GOD SHALL REVEAL UNTO ME THE SECRET OF GREAT SUCCESS!

People who normally rise to great heights are those who have more knowledge than others in their specific endeavors. You become more successful because you discover how to do certain things more effectively and successfully and also because you are able to access the secret things of life that separates you from others.

Jabez was born a reproach; his name which means 'Sorrow' was as a result of the circumstances of his birth. But when he discovered God in prayers, his destiny changed for good in 1 Chronicles 4:9-10. It is much the same with Daniel. One day he was a captive in Babylon, the next day he became a captain, strolling in the corridor of power with the princes of Persia because God revealed secret things to him. Daniel 2:18-19. I hereby prophesy, the LORD God of Daniel and Jabez shall reveal the secret to greatness to you in Jesus' mighty name. Amen!

When you discover the secret things, you move faster than others in the race of life. When you discover the secret things, you become confident in the steps you take in life. When you are equipped with the secret things of God, you circumvent harmful situations and take advantage of great opportunities even before other people become aware of them. Right now by the reason of the anointing, I release upon your life a greater knowledge of the secrets of God. The LORD God to grant you access to the secrets to great success in Jesus' name. Amen!

Prayer: *Holy Spirit! Open my spiritual understanding now!*

58

August 14th

The Word Today: Exodus 35:30-35

"And he hath filled him with the Spirit of God, in wisdom, in understanding, and in knowledge, and in all manner of workmanship; to devise curious works, to work in gold and in silver.........."

I AM ENDUED WITH THE GIFT TO ACHIEVE GREAT FEATS!

When God desires to achieve enormous exploits, He chooses human vessels with particular persona and bestows them with the ability to accomplish those feats. The chosen person becomes a personality of destiny. Bazeleel, the son of Uri was previously unknown in Israel until God chose him for the special assignment of building the tabernacle. After that event, the rest of the book of Exodus was dedicated to describing the works of Bazeleel hand. What an honor! I prophesy this day; the God of Bazeleel will honor you with a gift that will make a way of honor for you where there seems to be no way in Jesus' name. Amen!

God distinguished Bazeleel by giving him the enabling grace to execute the given task. That grace set him apart and on the path to success. It was grace that ensured that any person who had to learn that art had to train under him. That is what is called specialized skills. It is this special skill that enabled Bazeleel to accomplish that task. Saint, you are much more special to God than Bazeleel was. You are a new and special generation. God desired to make you great. So, I prophesy, today, the God of Bazeleel will give you the ability to accomplish great works in Jesus' name. Amen!

Prayer: *My Lord and My God I open my spirit, soul, and body unto you. Release that gifting for that special skill I need to accomplish uncommon feats in Jesus' name. Amen!*

I RECEIVE THE WINNING SPIRIT FROM THE LORD!

In his book "SCREW IT LET'S DO IT", the founding Chairman of 'Virgin Group' Richard Branson wrote; *"When I first discovered that my nickname among some members of staff at Virgin was 'Dr. Yes', I was amused. Obviously, it had come about because my automatic response to a question, a request, or a problem is more likely to be positive than negative. I have always tried to find reasons to do something if it seems like a good idea than not do it."*

Mr. Branson had the winning spirit; the power that propels men to great and greater heights. Wherever and whenever great works are achieved the winning spirit has played a major role. That is exactly what Joshua and Caleb exhibited in today's passage above. Whereas the rest of the people were scared by the challenge represented by the giants, he was spurring the people to go and take God's word of promise for it. Do you have such spirit in you? If not you need to pray for heaven to release it upon your life! You have to pray for the 'winning spirit' to come upon you or else it is practically impossible to achieve any major success in life with a layback attitude. David also had that spirit in him. That is why he saw Goliath as a giant opportunity while others saw him as a giant obstacle. Do you really need that grace in your life? I prophesy that the winning spirit is released upon you now! Go now and take dominion in all your endeavors in Jesus' mighty name. Amen!

Prayer: *Lord Jesus! Release upon me the supernatural grace that propels men to great height and success in Jesus' name.*

WORD SWORD OF THE ORACLE

The Word Today: Genesis 3:15 (NKJV)

*"And I will put enmity between you and the woman, and between your seed and her **Seed;** He shall bruise your head, and you shall bruise His heel."*

SEED [HEBREW] *ZERA*

The Hebrew word *Zera*, i.e. Seed in English as used in Genesis 3:15, Genesis 13:15, Genesis 22:18, Genesis 28:13, Psalm 89:4 as referenced in Strong's concordance #2233. The word translated seed can literally mean sown seed in the ground. Genesis 1:11-12 or figuratively one's offspring or descendants. Genesis 13:15. The word can refer also to a large group of people, such as the descendants of Abraham or a nation as in the nation of Israel, or it may refer to an individual.

In some parts of Genesis it refers specifically to the coming Messiah, as God's promised that the woman's 'Seed' would defeat the serpent in Genesis 3:15, see also Numbers 24:7, Isaiah 6:13, Galatians 3:16. As such, the term seed takes on great importance in the Bible. It is through the seed of Abraham, both collectively in Israel and specifically or singularly in Christ Jesus, that God would reach out to save all people Genesis 15:3.

Here are some Bible verses about Seed

1. Genesis 1:29 *"And God said, Behold, I have given you every herb bearing seed, which [is] upon the face of all the earth, and every tree, in the which [is] the fruit of a tree yielding seed; to you it shall be for meat."*

2. 1 Corinthians 15:38 *"But God giveth it a body as it hath pleased him, and to every seed his own body."*

61

CHURCH AND HOME SUNDAY SCHOOL

THE SECOND COMMANDMENT

WHAT IS THE SECOND COMMANDMENT?

"You shall not make for yourself a carved image—any likeness of anything that is in heaven above, or that is in the earth beneath, or that is in the water under the earth; Exodus 20:4 (NKJV)

WHAT DOES THE SECOND COMMANDMENT FORBID?

It forbids us to make any likeness of anything that is in heaven above, or in the earth beneath or in the water under the earth. We are forbidden to bow down to idols or serve them. We are forbidden to love and worship the good things of life more than God.

"For of this you can be sure: No immoral, impure or greedy person—such a person is an idolater—has any inheritance in the kingdom of Christ and of God." Ephesians 5:5 (NIV)

WHY DOES GOD FORBID IDOLATRY?

God forbids idolatry because God is a jealous God and will not share His glory or praise with anyone or anything.

"You shall not bow down to them nor serve them. For I, the Lord your God, am a jealous God, visiting the iniquity of the fathers upon the children to the third and fourth generations of those who hate Me." Exodus 20:5 (NKJV)

"I am the Lord, that is My name; And My glory I will not give to another, Nor My praise to carved images." Isaiah 42:8

SUNDAY SCHOOL QUESTIONS

Q1. WHAT IS THE SECOND COMMANDMENT?
Q2. WHAT DOES THE SECOND COMMANDMENT FORBID? Q3. WHY DOES GOD FORBID IDOLATRY?

Today's Memory Verse
"You shall not make for yourself a carved image—any likeness of anything that is in heaven above, or that is in the earth beneath, or that is in the water under the earth; Exodus 20:4 (NKJV)

Prayers:

1. *T*hank God for what He has done for you this far.
2. Thank You Lord for Your mercy endures forever.
3. Thank You O God for taking away every idol from my heart in the name of Jesus!
4. Lord! Let frustration and disappointment, be the portion of every object fashioned against me, in Jesus' name.
5. Every tie to polluted objects and family idol, break now by fire in the name of Jesus. Amen!
6. I crush any power given the mandate to hinder my progress physically and spiritually in Jesus' name. Amen!
7. Every curse that I have brought upon my life through ignorance and disobedience, break now by fire!
8. You power of sin magnetizing me physically and spiritually, I raise the blood of Jesus against you now.
9. Father! Separate my heart from any idol in Jesus' name!
10. Father Lord! Turn all my self-imposed curses to blessings.
11. Thank You O God for prayer answered.

The Word Today: Ezekiel 37:7-11

"... breathe upon these slain, that they may live. So I prophesied as he commanded me, and the breath came into them, and they lived, and stood up upon their feet, an exceeding great army."

EVERYTHING DEAD IN ME IS COMING BACK TO LIFE!

Preceding our text-passage above was a large army slain in the valley. They were rotted. They became dry bones, but God stepped in and reversed the irreversible and brought back to life an army that was already dead! I pray that every good thing in your life that is dead the LORD God shall bring them back to life this season in Jesus' powerful name. Amen!

Whatsoever you are dealing with right now, whatsoever situation you are facing in life, whether it is in your marriage, in your family, your business, in your Job place, in your community, politically, socially, economically, and in the entertainment arena. Be it in the judicial system. Whatsoever that has been put in place to function against your destiny today, I speak in God's stead, as His Oracle, and I declare the irreversible reversed now in the name of Jesus Christ; I decree a permanent solution to all your desolation in Jesus' mighty name. Amen!

You are created for a purpose whether the devil and his cohorts like it or not, from henceforth you will start fulfilling your purpose in life in the name of Jesus. Amen!

Prayer: *O God of the Oracle, reverse the irreversible in my life; change the unchangeable and make all impossibility become possible in Jesus' name. Amen!*

The Word Today: 2 Kings 1:13-14

EVERY AGENT OF DARKNESS SENT AGAINST ME SHALL FALL!

*W*ithout a doubt, Elijah was one man of God that understood his covenant rights. If only every believer could be as bold as he was, then Christian living would be more enjoyable. Twice King Ahaziah sent a company of fifty soldiers to man-handle and bundle the Prophet to the palace and twice he called down fire from heaven to consume them. In fear of the power of God on Elijah, the third Captain that was sent, fell down before him and pleaded for mercy. I prophesy the agent of destruction sent against you shall beg for your mercy in the name of Jesus. Amen!

There is one attribute that causes the powers of darkness to be afraid of Believers and that attribute is the fire power of the anointing. It is that fire that the Captain saw upon Elijah that made him bow. That 'Fire of the Anointing' can be acquired by fasting and praying. When a Believer embarks on fasting and prayer according to the will of God, the glory of God descends upon him in the form of a spiritual fire. This fire which is only visible to the spiritual eyes forms a ring of protection around you. It is this impregnable ring of protection that makes the enemy afraid of you. That ring was upon Elijah and that is why he was a terror to the forces of darkness. Today, by the virtue of my walk with God, that ring is upon me. By the power of transference, I hereby transfer that ring of protection upon you in Jesus' name. Amen! Henceforth, the powers of darkness and the gates of hell shall not prevail over you! They shall be scared of you in Jesus' name! You shall become too hot for them.

Prayer: *I receive the protective fire of God upon my life!*

The Word Today: 2 Chronicles 1:1-7

GOD WILL GIVE UNTO ME AN OPEN CHECK!

"And Solomon went up there to the bronze altar before the Lord, which was at the tabernacle of meeting, and offered a thousand burnt offerings on it. On that night God appeared to Solomon, and said to him, "Ask! What shall I give you?" Verse 6-7

Many actually believe that King Solomon was very fortunate. That it amounts to unusual favor for a person to receive the kind of special treatment Solomon had from God. Solomon had all the good things life could offer a person on a platter of gold.

I would not fault the fact that Solomon was favored by God; but I believe that Solomon actually deserved what he got. Imagine the cost of a thousand burnt offerings: the fund, the time and energy put in for the sacrifice unto God. Solomon was a record breaker. Compared to what David and all others before him used as offering, Solomon really shook the heavens with his sweet smelling offering. Consequently, because the LORD is a covenant keeping God, He had to give Solomon preferential treatment. You too can also appropriate the blessings of Solomon to yourself. God is bound by His words. In Genesis 8:22, He stated the key to wealth. Do you desire wealth? Learn to sow without ceasing and without measure if you desire abundant wealth. Do you desire an open check from God? Learn to sow an earth and heaven shaking seed like Solomon did. As you do so, God will give you an open check!

Prayer: *Lord! Give me the grace to sow abundantly to release my blessings in Jesus' name. Amen!*

EVERY COUNSEL OF THE WICKED FOR MY LIFE IS NULLIFIED!

The sum of our text-passage above is that God does not support those who oppress others. For that reason, He always nulls and voids every counsel of the wicked against the righteous. So, as a Child of God, you should be assured that every counsel of the enemy against you is nullified in the name of Jesus. I want you to know that as you desire and plan good things for your life, so also are the wicked planning evil for you. You do not need to have done anything wrong against anyone before they start attacking you. The mere fact that you are living as a child of God is enough to provoke the wrath of the Satan the enemy.

However, according to the scripture, the plans of your enemies, their machinations, and actions etc., cannot determine the outcome of your life because God has the final say. I may not know what the enemy has planned or is doing in your life right now. Maybe they have been doing incantations to cause failure in your endeavor. They may be doing enchantments and divinations to ensure that you do not manifest the glory of God. Whatever it is they are doing against you, I want you to know this day that they have already failed even before they started. Because if God said there shall be no enchantment and divination against you; meaning every weapon form or fashioned against you will not prosper. They will eventually fail in the name of Jesus. Amen! I pray for you now, every instrument of evil issued against you are hereby destroyed!

Prayer: *By the reason of the anointing every yoke in my life is broken in the name of Jesus Christ. Amen!*

The Word Today: Daniel 1:1-4

"...... bring certain of the children of Israel, and of the king's seed, and of the princes; Children with no blemish, but well favored, and skilful in all wisdom and cunning in knowledge, and understanding science, and such as had ability in them to stand in the king's palace......."

THE LORD GOD WILL SET ME APART FOR DIVINE LIFTING!

Several Jewish youth were taken captive from Jerusalem to Babylon but only a few were set apart for the king's service. They included Daniel and the popular Hebrew trio: Shedrach Meshach and Abednego. So, these four were set on the path to greatness even while they were still youngsters. I prophesy, this day the LORD God will set you apart for greatness in Jesus' mighty name. Amen!

Nevertheless, these youths did not achieve their respectable status by chance. They worked for it. The Bible recorded that they were wise, knowledgeable, informed and educated. This means if you desire to be set apart, for greatness, you have to be prepared for it, you must work hard for it, and you can't be lazy. As the saying goes, "fate favors the prepared mind."

Do you desire greatness? Prepare for it. 2 Timothy 2:15 says *"Study to show thyself approved unto God, a workman that needeth not to be ashamed, rightly dividing the word of truth."* Study, pray, live right and position yourself for greatness. The Lord will set you apart for greatness in Jesus' name. Remain Blessed!

Prayer: Lord! Put an excellent spirit in me. Set me apart O Lord for greatness in Jesus' name. Amen!

WORD SWORD OF THE ORACLE

The Word Today: Genesis 37:5

---

*"Now Joseph had a **dream**, and he told it to his brothers; and they hated him even more."*

DREAM [HEBREW] *CHALOM*

*D*ream, *Chalom* in Hebrew as used in our text-verse above and in other Bible verses like Gen. 40:5, Gen. 41:7, Joel 2:28 Strong's concordance #2472. The Hebrew word *Chalom* simply means "to dream". The ancients understand a dream or a vision of the night as "watching during sleep" this suggest a special state of consciousness. Often dreams were recognized as revelations from the gods, or from the LORD God Himself in the case of the Hebrews understanding. Many times these dreams and visions were encoded in symbolic language that needed decoding, and interpretation. Those who could interpret dreams are powerful people in the ancient world Gen. 41:37-43, Dan. 2:46-49. Joseph not only dreams, but also was gifted in dreams interpretation. He receives message in dreams and also interpret such messages. He was able to interpret the figures and metaphors of dream-event as God enabled him to. Gen. 40:8, Gen. 41:16.

Here are some Bible verses on Dreams:

Job 33:14-18, Eccl. 5:3, Dan. 5:12, Jer. 23:28, Eccl. 5:7, Dan. 1:17, Dan. 2:19, Job 4:12-21, Prov. 25:2, 1 Kings 3:3-15, Acts 2:17, Matt. 2:13, Zech. 10:2, Habakkuk 2:2, Dan. 7, Dan. 2:28-30, Ps. 16:7, Gen. 41:15-16, Acts 23:11, Acts 16:9, Matt. 27:19, Matt. 2:19-22, Matt. 1:20, Dan. 2:47, Dan. 2:16-23, Jer. 29:8, Jer. 23:25-32, Isa. 29:7, Job 20:8, Judg. 7:13, Gen. 46:2, Gen. 41:25-32, Gen. 40:8-23, Gen. 31:24 Gen. 31:10-13, Gen. 28:12 Gen. 20:3, Acts 10:10-16, Acts 10:3-6 Joel 2:28, Jer. 27:9, Isa. 29:8

CHURCH AND HOME SUNDAY SCHOOL

HOW DOES GOD LOOK UPON IDOLATRY?

God looks at idolatry as degrading, the practice of fools and abomination in His sight.

"Therefore, since we are the offspring of God, we ought not to think that the Divine Nature is like gold or silver or stone, something shaped by art and man's devising." Acts 17:29 (NKJV)

"Professing to be wise, they became fools, and changed the glory of the incorruptible God into an image made like corruptible man—and birds and four-footed animals and creeping things." Romans 1:22-23 (NKJV)

WHAT IS AN ABOMINATION?

An abomination is an idolatrous sin that incites the wrath of God upon man. And the wrath of God is God's reaction to unrighteousness and sinfulness.

"When you come into the land which the Lord your God is giving you, you shall not learn to follow the abominations of those nations. There shall not be found among you anyone who makes his son or his daughter pass through the fire, or one who practices witchcraft, or a soothsayer, or one who interprets omens, or a sorcerer, or one who conjures spells, or a medium, or a spiritist, or one who calls up the dead. For all who do these things are an abomination to the Lord, and because of these abominations the Lord your God drives them out from before you." Deuteronomy 18:9-12 (NKJV)

"You shall burn the carved images of their gods with fire; you shall not covet the silver or gold that is on them, nor take it for

yourselves, lest you be snared by it; for it is an abomination to the Lord your God." Deuteronomy 7:25

HOW CAN WE PLEASE GOD AND SECURE HIS BLESSINGS?

1. By serving the only 'True God' Matthew 22:36-40.

2. By worshiping Him in spirit and in truth John 4:24-25.

3. Love God and your neighbors as yourself Mark 12:30-31.

4. By obeying and doing His will. John 14:15.

5. By faith Hebrews 11:6.

SUNDAY SCHOOL QUESTIONS

Q1. HOW DOES GOD LOOK UPON IDOLATRY?
Q2. WHAT IS AN ABOMINATION?
Q3. HOW CAN WE PLEASE GOD AND SECURE HIS BLESSINGS?

Today's Memory Verse:
John 14:15 (NKJV) *"If you love Me, keep My commandments."*

Today's Prayers:

1. *Thank God for His love and His word for your life!*
2. *Lord! Help me love You and my neighbor as myself*
3. *Deliver me Lord from the abomination of this land in the name of Jesus. Amen!*
4. *Father let my life and my living be pleasing unto You.*
5. *Help me serve and worship You in spirit and in truth!*

The Word Today: Isaiah 28:16

I BELIEVE SO I SHALL RECEIVE: DELAY IS NOT DENIAL!

Praise God! The testimony below will encourage you: This woman for 18 years was waiting for the fruit of the womb, she made the home of the herbalist and fertility clinic her inhabitation and she took all kinds of medications and concoction of different types for over ten years. At that time she has not known Christ, but then she later got saved and was still trusting God, and within a short time, God answered her prayer and the evidence of the answered prayer is a set of twins. Glory to God! Alleluia! Hear her:

"I don't know how to say it, I don't know what to say but it is the miracle of God! In my 18 years experience in barrenness ... I really suffered; running from place to place, looking for peace. I have no peace. Every day I lamented. I prayed, calling on God to help me. I went here and there looking for the fruit of the womb for 18 years but when the miracle of God came, really it did not waste time. Someone told me to join the prayer line of the Oracle of God Int'l Ministries. According to her, that was the place that worked for her; I said no I will not; there is no place I have not gone to, so I will not. The lady literally forced me to join! After a couple of weeks I join the prayer line and that was the end of my reproach. That very month, I missed my period; today my babies, a boy and a girl are two months old and I will be 49 years old next November! God did it! And with God it did not take time! I took-in the first night Rev. Stevie declared it in Jesus' name. Praise the Lord! Alleluia!" Sister J.

Prayer: *I believe delay is not denial so I will surely testify!*

"Now the Lord is the Spirit; and where the Spirit of the Lord is, there is liberty."

I AM LIBERATED BY THE SPIRIT OF THE LORD!

What is it, that has held you and your family bound generationally? What affliction has the enemy used to oppress you for this long? What is the negativity that you and your loved ones have been dealing with all these years in your lineage? Is it premature death? Is it miscarriages, singleness, bareness, stagnancy and inexplicable misfortune? Whatever it is, as the LORD God lives, I declare your deliverance and liberty this day in Jesus' name. The only thing left for you to do now, is to give your life to Jesus! If you are born again you must liberate your mindset concerning your situation and you will begin to experience mighty changes in every area of your life. The spiritual rebirth will engraft you by faith to the lineage of Abraham. This, by implication makes you a spiritual Jew who is heir to the Abrahamic covenant. The new covenant automatically nulls and voids the old order on which you have been operating, in your earthly lineage or bloodline.

Have you been under the influence of curses? This is your day of liberation. Take your case now to the court of heaven and remind God that the covenant of your new birth has destroyed that of the old. Romans 11:16-18. As you do so in prayer and faith, the power of liberation that is ever present in the blood of Jesus will surely step into your every situation and cause every curse to be broken and you shall receive your deliverance in the mighty name of Jesus Christ. Amen!

Prayer: *Lord Jesus! I thank You for my liberation this day!*

The Word Today: Judges 11:1-11

THOSE WHO DERIDE ME SHALL SURELY CELEBRATE ME!

Jephthah's story was indeed very interesting and instructive. At one point, he was a despised son of a prostitute. No one wanted anything to do with him. His siblings and the entire land rejected and disinherited him. And then shortly after, he became the leader of street rogues. But before long, the LORD God arranged a situation to lift him up, those who loathed him came together to make him their leader. That is how it is when God marks you for divine lifting. And as you read this; receive the anointing for divine lifting now in the name of Jesus! I prophesy those who deride you now will celebrate you soon in the mighty name of Jesus. Amen!

In my early days in ministry, many people who could not envision and discern the plan of God for me ridiculed me; some wondered aloud why I fasted so much, others concluded I couldn't get far in ministry. In fact it was a wilderness experience. But God turned this thing around for me like He did for Jephthah and David. Alleluia! Today many who avoided me like I was a plague now scramble for appointments to see or speak with me or have me speak. The God that did it for me will do likewise for you. He is the same yesterday, today and forever. Are you despised right now for your race or lineage? Is it because of the circumstances surrounding your birth or because of an unfortunate situation in your life? Saint, do not stop believing God for a turnaround miracle. For those who despise you now will surely celebrate you soon in Jesus' name!

Prayer: *O God of Jephthah lift me above my adversaries!*

August 28th

The Word Today: Matthew 27:15-26

"... Then answered all the people, and said, His blood be on us, and on our children. Then released he, Barabbas unto them: and........he delivered him to be crucified".

I DECREE! MY RELEASE INTO MY DESTINY!

𝐵arabbas was a hardened criminal. He's been tried and condemned to death for his crimes. He was on death row. But when Jesus took his place, Barabbas became a free man. As such, no power on earth could arrest him after that. This is a graphic illustration of the ministry of Our Lord and Savior Jesus Christ on earth. The same way He took the place of Barabbas and freed him, so also He took our place on the "Cross of Calvary".

As a result, just like Barabbas, we are free to live our life according to the will of God, free from the dominion of sin, free from satanic oppressions and affliction, because all the powers that have held us bound have lost their legal grounds. Therefore, I prophesy, you are released into your destiny in the mighty name of Jesus. Amen!

The powers that have held you bound in custody are destroyed by the power in the covenant blood of Jesus, shed at the "Cross of Calvary". That blood was shed for the remission of your sins. Therefore, no devil, no demon, sickness or disease or fear can hold you bound. Once again, by the power in the blood, you are released into your divine destiny in Jesus' name. Amen!

Prayer: *By the authority and power in the blood of Jesus Christ, I declare that I am released into my destiny in Jesus' name!*

75

The Word Today: Exodus 14:1-4

THE LORD GOD SHALL BE GLORIFIED IN MY SITUATION!

If the Israelites had known God's plan for them, perhaps they would have been less afraid of Pharaoh's Pursuit. If they knew that God had arranged the circumstances of the Red Sea dilemma to the demise of their enemies, they would not have cried and wailed as much as they did when they were in between the Red Sea and the army of Egypt. But they did not. That is why they cried like hopeless people in their persecution. Imagine what God thought as He watched them wail like people who had no helper as Pharaoh threatened. That is exactly how God feels many times when He sees us complaining endlessly about the difficulties of our lives.

In our word above, it is obvious that God arranged the pursuit of Pharaoh and the difficulties of that situation for His own glory. He used the situation to teach everyone that He is most powerful. By defeating and destroying Pharaoh and the Egyptian army, He was established as the ultimate power in existence then and forever; not that He needed to, but He chose to! Today like in the past, God is still in the habit of proving Himself to confirm His word mightily in the lives of Believers. That is why He allows certain situations in our lives. He allows such trials and tribulations to precede your total triumph and victory so that we can appreciate Him more. What challenge are you facing today? I want you to know that it is not for worst. Just, look up with hope and faith because God will be glorified in every one of your situations in Jesus' name. Amen!

Prayer: *God will be glorified in every adverse situation in my life.*

WORD SWORD OF THE ORACLE

The Word Today: Genesis 41:1 (NKJV)

*"Then it came to pass, at the end of two full years, that **Pharaoh** had a dream; and behold, he stood by the river."*

PHARAOH [HEBREW] *PAR 'OH*

Par 'oh is the Hebrew word for Pharaoh as applied in Genesis 41:1, Strong's concordance #6547. The name Pharaoh comes from the Egyptian word *Pr-'o*, which means "the great house." Originally the word Pharaoh was not a designation for the king of Egypt, but a reference to his palace. The ancient Egyptians believed that Pharaoh was a living representation of the god Horus in Egyptian religion, identified with the cult of the sun god and symbolized by the falcon.

The plagues against the Egyptians prior to the exodus of the Children of Israel from Egypt were cosmic in nature; it was a kind of spiritual warfare between the living God and the false gods of Egypt. Exodus 12:12, Exodus 15:11. The tenth plague, cumulating in the death of the firstborn among the Egyptians, including Pharaoh's, was divine judgment upon Pharaoh's claim to deity. Exodus 12:29-30, Exodus 18:11-12.

Some Bible verses about Pharaoh

Genesis 39:1-23, Exodus 14:8, Exodus 4:21, Exodus 14:4, Exodus 11:10, Exodus 10:20, Exodus 10:1, Exodus 9:34-35, Exodus 9:12, Exodus 8:32, Exodus 8:19, Exodus 7:22, 2 Timothy 3:8, Romans 9:17, Exodus 14:17, Exodus 12:29, Exodus 11:1-10, and Exodus 7:1.

5th Sunday of the Month of August

CHURCH AND HOME SUNDAY SCHOOL

THE THIRD COMMANDMENT

WHAT IS THE THIRD COMMANDMENT?

"You shall not take the name of the Lord your God in vain, for the Lord will not hold him guiltless who takes His name in vain." Exodus 20:7 (NKJV)

WHAT IS MEANT BY TAKING GOD'S NAME IN VAIN?

It is when the name of God or that of Jesus Christ is used to attribute an act or statement to God that is not of God. It is also sinful to use God thoughtlessly in uncertain or unimportant matters or to express surprise, anger and frustration.

WHAT IS COMMANDED BY THE THIRD COMMANDMENT?

We are commanded to always speak with reverence of God and to be truthful at all times and especially when we take oaths or making vows and pledges. We should be known by our wholesome conversation that reflects the work of grace in our hearts.

"Nor should there be obscenity, foolish talk or coarse joking, which are out of place, but rather thanksgiving." Ephesians 5:4 (NIV)

WHAT DOES THE THIRD COMMANDMENT FORBID?

It forbids us to speak irreverently of God, to take the name of God as witness without necessity, to take an oath to something that is false or to break a lawful oath. It forbids us to make a vow falsely or break a sacred vow. Blasphemy, cursing, using witchcraft, lying or deceiving by God's name are also prohibited.

"Again you have heard that it was said to those of old, 'You shall not swear falsely, but shall perform your oaths to the Lord.' But I say to you, do not swear at all: neither by heaven, for it is God's throne; nor by the earth, for it is His footstool; nor by Jerusalem, for it is the city of the great King. Nor shall you swear by your head, because you cannot make one hair white or black. But let your 'Yes' be 'Yes,' and your 'No,' 'No.' for whatever is more than these is from the evil one." Matthew 5:33-37 (NKJV)

SUNDAY SCHOOL QUESTIONS

Q1. WHAT IS THE THIRD COMMANDMENT?
Q2. WHAT IS MEANT BY TAKING GOD'S NAME IN VAIN?
Q3. WHAT IS COMMANDED BY THE THIRD COMMANDMENT? Q4. WHAT DOES THE THIRD COMMANDMENT FORBID?

Memory Verse:
"You shall not take the name of the Lord your God in vain, for the Lord will not hold him guiltless who takes His name in vain." Exodus 20:7 (NKJV)

Prayers

1. *Thank You Lord for Your word in my life!*
2. *Forgive me for ever using Your name in vain in the name of Jesus.*

The Word Today: Psalm 67:3-7

I PROPHESY! MY PRAISE SHALL TRIGGER MY DELIVERANCE!

In Act 16:16-26 Paul and Silas must have prayed and fasted for days. And on the night preceding the morning of their execution; Paul told Silas, 'we've fasted enough, we've prayed enough, we had vigils, now let us praise God.' As they did an earthquake occurred and their chains where broken, the gates of the prison fell flat and the angel of God led them out of captivity in the eleventh hour. Do you want freedom? Praise God mightily now!

PRAISE THE LORD NOW!

Father! I give You glory, honor and adoration. You are worthy to be praised! Glory be to Your Holy name Lord, I praise and magnify Your Holy name. You are worthy to be adored and magnified, I give You all the glory Lord, You are the king of kings and the Lord of lords, the ancient of days, the Rock of ages, our help in ages past, our hope for years to come, the I am that I am, the unchangeable Lord, the unchangeable changer, the impossibility made possible God, You reverse the irreversible, the only one who never sleeps nor slumbers. I bless Your holy name! Thank You Lord Jesus. Accept my worship in Jesus' name. Amen!

SEPTEMBER BIRTHDAY AND WEDDING ANNIVERSARY PRAYERS!

Father, I commit Your September children and those celebrating their marriage this month into Your everlasting hands: this is the month of fruitfulness, let them be fruitful in the name of Jesus.

80

THE LABOR ROOM OF SEPTEMBER PART 1

The ninth month of the year is a very significant month because of inherent powers in the number 9. The ninth month, which is the first month of remembrance, is a turn-around month if handled properly and spiritually. One of the properties and characteristics of the ninth month is the fact that it is the gestation period for human pregnancy. Human pregnancy from conception to full term is nine months. The forces of darkness and wickedness tap into this truth to control, steal, kill and destroy many destinies. We have a spiritual obligation to make September produce a bundle of joyful testimonies for us if we know what to do and do it.

September in another sense is what I call, the "LABOUR-ROOM MONTH", because after full term gestation period, certain things, either positive or negative must be birthed. If you have ever been to the maternity ward, the most common language of the labor room is 'PUSH!' I now welcome you to the LABOR ROOM of September. In spiritual warfare, PUSH means 'Pray Until Something Happens'. (P.U.S.H). So PUSH is the battle cry of prayer warriors in the spiritual labor room of September.

September is not just a month; but a personality with a womb. The bible tells us in Psalm 110:3 that morning is a personality with a womb, not just a natural entity. Today you must sow a positive seed into the womb of September by prophetically praying thus: *Thou womb of September, produce a bundle of joyful testimonies for me in the name of Jesus. Amen!*

Many months were named after idols. For example, January was named after the Greek goddess of the sun, Janus. If you carelessly enter January which was consecrated by those who worshipped the Sun, the elements could be used to control your life throughout that year. They could command the sun to smite you by day and the moon by night. No month is a natural entity. You must program better and glorious things into them, if you must live a fulfilled life. Don't be a careless and naive Believer! There are three possibilities in the physical labor room.

1. The pregnant woman goes in, and comes out with an additional bundle of joy called a child or children, if the babies are twins, triplets, etc. That is a positive multiplication;

2. The pregnant woman goes in, and comes out alone, with a sad subtraction – no child due to still-birth or other tragic complications during childbirth. *This will not be your lot in Jesus' name. Amen!*

3. The third possibility is the tragic maternal mortality of when a pregnant woman goes in but neither child nor mother comes out alive. This is the reason why many tremble with trepidation as the Expected Delivery Date (EDD) approaches.

Pray now these prayers:

1. *Blood of Jesus fight for me in the labor room of September of this year in the name of Jesus. Amen!*

2. *September is my Expected Delivery Date, therefore, O God Arise! Protect and defend my harvest of great testimonies, in the name of Jesus. Amen!*

3. *Every power waiting to abort my miracle at the time of my testimonies. You are a liar die by fire in the name of Jesus!*

82

September 3rd

The Word Today: Isaiah 66:7-9

THE LABOR ROOM OF SEPTEMBER PART 2

Saint! You need to know that every prayer warrior is a midwife of the midnight season. I wish you would add the fireworks of the September labor room to your arsenal of midnight hour 'Fire-full' prayers for the remaining days in your September. No midwife goes to sleep in the labor room, else that slumber can cause tragic consequences. The labor room is a theater of battle.

There are evil powers that allow people to dream and nurture testimonies but wait for them at the maturity date to shatter those beautiful dreams. So be vigilant! Just like the physical labor room of any maternity, the following nine things, among many others, are characteristics of September:

1. The labor room of September is a place of expectations both positive and negative, *the choice is yours to make.*
2. It is a place of conflict and warfare you must fight or you are finish. *(The choice is yours to make).*
3. The labor room of September is a place of life and death. *(The choice is yours to make).*
4. The labor room of September is a place of joy and sadness. *(The choice is yours to make).*
5. It is a place of fear and faith *the choice is yours to make.*
6. The labor room of September is a place of addition and subtraction. *(The choice is yours to make).*
7. The labor room of September is a place of harvest.
8. The labor room of September is a place where the spiritual midwife (that is, the intercessors) is in charge.
9. The labor room of September is a place of the blood.

83

PRAYER POINTS

1. The pregnancy of good news conceived for my sake shall not be aborted, shall not be miscarried and shall not be still-birth, therefore, my testimony be birthed alive now in Jesus' name.

2. You pregnancy of wickedness conceived against my destiny, in the womb of September, perish now in the name of Jesus.

3. Dark expectations for my destiny be aborted now by fire!

4. Thou womb of September, hear the word of the Lord: bring forth my turn-around breakthroughs in the name of Jesus.

5. Witchcraft powers waiting for my loss in the labor room of September, you are a liar perish now by fire in Jesus' name!

6. Witchcraft powers waiting for my death in the labor room of September, you are a LIAR! Perish in my stead in Jesus' name!

7. September is my Expected Delivery Date, therefore, O God Arise! Protect and defend my harvest of great testimonies.

8. Every power waiting for my failure, hear the word of the Lord: You shall wait in vain in the name of Jesus. Amen!

9. Evil power assigned to assault me at the edge of my breakthrough I am not your candidate. Therefore perish!

10. Evil power programmed to drain the battery of my destiny, you are a liar! I paralyze you now in the name of Jesus. Amen!

11. Unfriendly friends! Lose your power over my life and perish in the name of Jesus. Amen!

12. Wrath of God, strike through every evil king that presides over my September, in the name of Jesus. Amen!

13. There shall be no error in the labor room of my breakthrough in the name of Jesus. Amen!

14. I paralyze every evil midwife in the labor room of my breakthrough in the name of Jesus. Amen!

15. Powers of failure at the edge of my breakthrough break now in the name of Jesus. Amen!

The Word Today: Ecclesiastes 7:11-12 (NKJV)

I WILL NOT SQUANDER MY INHERITANCE WHEN RESTORED!

Jesus Christ knew a lot about money. And He was not ashamed of talking about it. If you add up all of the parables that Jesus spoke, most of them are about money! Because Jesus knew what we all know - that the way to a man's heart is not necessarily his stomach but his wallet! Jesus knew that our relationship with money is really a reflection of our relationship with God. So since He came to bridge the gap between man and God, it only makes sense that He needed to deal with this money issue that is on everyone's mind at all times.

One of my favorite Jesus parables about money is that of the prodigal son. Now, maybe you don't quite view that parable in terms of money. Maybe you think of it as a tale of love, forgiveness and the mercy of God. It is all of those things, but even more so, it is a picture of two brothers, who each handled money differently. One handled money God's way and the other didn't. Luke 15:11-32. Basically, the younger brother wanted it all and he wanted it now. The Father, being too generous - gave him his portion. However, soon through reckless living he squandered all of it and landed in the 'pig's pen' so to say. When he came to his senses, the younger brother returned and the Father forgave him and embraced him as a son again. The older brother was upset. He had been working and doing all the right things all this time. What was the point of it all then? And the Father said in verse 31 *"Son, you are always with me, and all that is mine is yours."*

Pray thus:

Prayer: *Lord Jesus! Open my spiritual understanding to prosper!*

The Word Today: Esther 5:1-2; Esther 4:1-7

"....... And it was so, when the king saw Esther the queen standing in the court, that she obtained favour in his sight....."

I PROPHESY! PROCEDURES WILL BE SET ASIDE TO FAVOR ME!

*H*istorical records show King Ahasuerus was a very spontaneous man. History has it that he once ordered the sea be flogged three hundred lashes or strokes of the cane because the bridge he built over it collapsed. He was highly impulsive. No wonder, he had his wife Queen Vashti deposed and exiled for refusing to do a strip show before him and his acolytes.

One would expect that, a man with such unstable character would have instantly ordered the death of Esther for daring to come into his presence without invitation; against the law of the land. But that was not to be. Against all odds and expectations, Ahasuerus set protocol aside and raised the scepter to admit Esther into his presence. Breaking; all policy, protocol and procedure of the palace to save Esther.

Surely, such miracle can only happen to God's favored people. Today, like Esther, God has decided to favor you. So I prophesy wherever you go, unfavorable procedures, protocols and policy will be set aside to favor you in the name of Jesus. The angel called favor, the angel named goodness and mercy shall follow and go before you all the days of your life and you shall dwell in the house of the LORD forever. Amen!

Prayer: *"O God! Cause men and women to set aside protocols and procedure to bless me in Jesus' name. Amen!"*

WORD SWORD OF THE ORACLE

The Word Today: Genesis 17:1 (NKJV) .

---

*"When Abram was ninety-nine years old, the Lord appeared to Abram and said to him, "I am **Almighty** God; walk before Me and be blameless."*

ALMIGHTY [HEBREW] *SHADDAI*

𝒯he Hebrew word *"Shaddai"* as used in the above text-verse and in Gen. 28:3, Gen. 35:11, Gen. 43:14, Gen. 48:3, Gen. 49:25, and Job 37:23 Strong's #7706 means 'Almighty'. The divine name is *'EL-Shaddai'*. *El* means God from the Hebrew word *Elohim* and *Shaddai* is related to the Akkadian word for 'mountain' or relative to a Hebrew verb meaning mighty. God is *"mountain-like."* He is Powerful, Majestic, Awe-inspiring, and Enduring. Just like a mountain, He provides shelter from the elements and from evil. Ps. 91:1-2. Therefore, *"El-Shaddai"* means *"Majestic Deity"* or the God Who Provides my Refuge."

The word "El" is the root of Elohim from which we get "mighty, power, omnipotence, The strong one." Ps. 18:2, Ps. 68:35. The name El describes God as the strength giver to His people. Shaddai is translated 48 times in the Bible as "Almighty," and 24 times as "Breast." El-Shaddai is described as the One who nourishes and supplies the needs of His people; the Almighty One who supplies and satisfies our needs. God is the All-Sufficient One. John 15:5. When we do not realize our total dependence on Him He purges or chastens us. El-Shaddai speaks of God's power, sufficiency, and the inexhaustible supply of God's riches and strength; it reminds us of His strength made perfect in our weakness and His fullness in our emptiness. Do we long to be filled with His power? Then ask now to be filled.

1ˢᵗ Sunday of the Month of September

CHURCH AND HOME SUNDAY SCHOOL

WHAT IS AN OATH?

An oath is calling on God to witness what we say as truth.

"And you shall not swear by My name falsely, nor shall you profane the name of your God: I am the Lord." Leviticus 19:12 (NKJV)

"Moreover I call God as witness against my soul, that to spare you I came no more to Corinth." 2 Corinthians 1:23 (NKJV)

WHEN ARE WE PERMITTED AND REQUIRED TO TAKE AN OATH?

We are permitted to take oath when:

a.   We are called upon by government; for example when witnesses are asked to testify in a court of law.
"Let every soul be subject to the governing authorities. For there is no authority except from God, and the authorities that exist are appointed by God." Romans 13:1 (NKJV)

b.   An oath is necessary for the glory of God or the welfare of our neighbor.

"You shall fear the Lord your God and serve Him, and shall take oaths in His name." Deuteronomy 6:13 (NKJV)

"For men indeed swear by the greater, and an oath for confirmation is for them an end of all disputes." Hebrews 6:16

BIBLE NARATIVES:

1.   ABRAHAM PUT HIS SERVANT UNDER OATH: Genesis 24:3-9

2. PAUL MADE AN OATH: 2 Corinthians 1:23

WHAT ARE THE THREE THINGS NECESSARY TO MAKE AN OATH?

1. There must be good reason for taking the oath.
2. There must be no doubt that what we say under oath is true and nothing but the truth.
3. An oath must never be taken to do what is wrong.

WHEN DOES AN OATH BECOME SINFUL?

An oath becomes sinful when it is taken falsely, thoughtlessly, or in sinful, uncertain or unimportant matters.

BIBLE NARATIVES:

1. PETER SWORE FALSELY: Matthew 26:72
2. CERTAIN JEWS SWORE TO MURDER PAUL: Acts 23:12
3. HEROD SWORE IN AN UNCERTAIN AND UNIMPORTANT MATTER: Mark 6:23

SUNDAY SCHOOL QUESTIONS

Q1. WHAT IS AN OATH?
Q2. WHEN ARE WE PERMITTED/ REQUIRED TO TAKE AN OATH?
Q3. WHAT ARE THE THREE NECESSITIES TO MAKE AN OATH?
Q4. WHEN DOES AN OATH BECOME SINFUL?

> **Memory Verse:** "You shall fear the Lord your God and serve Him, and shall take oaths in His name."
> Deuteronomy 6:13

The Word Today: Deuteronomy 8:18

I AM EMPOWERED TO BE WEALTHY!

*G*od's way of doing things is difference from ours. You can get the secret about receiving the power to get wealth if you ask God! The Scripture says the world's way leads to pain, sorrow and death. But God empowers you to gain wealth without pain and sorrow added to it! You are imparted with these powerful truths and anointing for prosperity; if you follow the flow of my teachings and do the word of God and not just reading and hearing the messages. You shall surely prosper in Jesus' name.

There is a way of doing things the world's way and then there is God's way. If you wonder why you are not experiencing the financial blessing that you are longing for, if you ever wonder why after you serve, sow seed of faith, tithe, fasted and prayed, and you still did not get the answer you have been looking for. You need to seek the anointing to get wealth from God! Stop doing the same thing and expect a different result. If you ever wondered why some people just seem to have it so easy and you are always struggling, you will find out the answer here. In this ministry; we make available to you the culmination of all that the Lord has taught us from His Word and by His Spirit. I truly and strongly believe, you will be set free from want if you follow through; and I know that the Lord's blessing will overtake you like an avalanche. As Believers we are meant to provoke the world to envy. When is the last time the world was envious of you because of your wealth? It is about time that you rise up and start walking in the fullness of the blessing of God!

Prayer: *Lord! Anoint me with the power to get wealth!*

The Word Today: Genesis 42:5-10

MY ENEMIES WILL NOT EXPERIENCE THEIR EXPECTATION!

Have you ever asked yourself why Joseph recognized his brothers immediately he saw them in verse 7 of today's word? And none of the ten brothers could recognize Joseph. You may argue that Joseph physical appearance and features may have changed. But I think the main reason they could not recognized him was because they did not find him where they expected him to be. If they had met him as a servant, they would have recognized him. If they had seen him in prison, they would have recognized him.

Indeed, I am sure that if the brothers of Joseph had met him struggling to survive, they would have called him by his first and nick name at first sight. But because in their wildest imagination they never thought that Joseph, the little boy they sold into slavery over a decade ago would be anywhere, near the governor of Egypt's residence. But there he was, Joseph, right before them, the governor of Egypt himself. Since they could not imagine him being there, they could not recognize him.

I don't know what your enemies have done against you. They may have conspired to destroy you and your dreams like they did to Joseph. They may have concluded that you will never amount to anything. But according to the word of God, I prophesy your enemies will not experience their expectation concerning you in the name of Jesus Christ. Amen!

Prayer: *This day I claim divine elevation and my enemies will not find me where they expected me to be in Jesus' name.*

The Word Today: Exodus 14:19-20

"And the Angel of God, who went before the camp of Israel, moved and went behind them; and the pillar of cloud went from before them and stood behind them. So it came between the camp of the Egyptians and the camp of Israel. Thus it was a cloud and darkness to the one, and it gave light by night to the other, so that the one did not come near the other all that night."

ADVERSE SITUATIONS IN MY LIFE WILL WORK OUT FOR GOOD!

I often counsel Believers that we are special in God's eyes. So conditions that are applicable to others do not necessarily apply to us. As a child of God, the fact that someone else failed in a particular business or career does not mean that we cannot succeed therein. So many Believers have lost their blessings because they become carried away by crowd mentality. Which make people barricade their minds to investment and ventures that might offer them great opportunities simply because someone else failed at such business. Such attitude is responsible for the destruction of many dreams and visions.

It is very instructive to note that as in the story in our Scripture above, what is applicable to one person might not necessarily happen or apply to another. In Exodus 14:20, the same pillar of cloud that put the camp of Egypt in darkness gave light to the Israelites. So, it was difference stroke for different folks. I don't know your mindset right now; but I prophesy that every adverse situation in your life will work out for good for you in Jesus' mighty name. Amen!

Prayer: *Everything adverse situation will work together for my good in Jesus' name. Amen!*

The Word Today: Jeremiah 18:1-6

In Mark 2:1-12 a man paralyzed from the neck down was carried to Jesus Christ; and the great potter spoke and said, "Get up, take your bed and go home." The man suddenly became whole again. No matter the nature of your sickness, God, the almighty Potter will repair you this day in Jesus' name. Amen!

And it doesn't matter how long the problem had been there. In John 5:1-9 the Bible tells us of a man who had been sick for 38 years. When the Lord Potter came, He spoke; and with His word of power, the one who has been sick for 38 years immediately became whole again. I don't care how long you have been sick the Almighty God will heal you today in Jesus' name. Amen! In 2 Kings 5:1-14, when God heal Naaman of leprosy, his skin became like the skin of a new born baby. You are going to get brand new parts from God this day in Jesus' name. Amen!

Three years ago in one of our revivals the word of God came while I was preaching that there was a man in the meeting, one of his kidney has been removed, the second kidney is also malfunctioning and the Lord said He has give him two brand new kidneys. The man who had that problem said, "AMEN!" the next day, he ran to the hospital and they did a test, and The Doctors said, "We remember this case, when we were removing one of the kidneys the surgery took several hours. But what am I seeing? This man should have one kidney but now he has two!" I decree this day you will get new heart, new eyes and new ear drums! New brain! New womb! New back-bones! Whatever you need new! If you believe it, then receive it now in Jesus' name!

Prayer: *O Lord! Give me a new life in the name of Jesus!*

93

"..... *Surely he hath borne our grief, and carried our sorrows: yet we did esteem him stricken, smitten of God, and afflicted. ...*"

THE LORD GOD SHALL CARRY MY BURDEN!

The lame man at the beautiful gate in the book of Acts of Apostle chapter number 3 was a burden to himself and his relatives. The Bible said they carried him daily for 40 years. That was a reproach right there, I'm sure he was even ashamed of himself, but there was nothing he could do about his situation. He was helpless and hopeless. There are some people who by now should be their own landlords or home owners, but they are still living at the mercy of their landlords. In that name that is above every other name, you will move to your own house this year in the name of Jesus. Amen!

For 40 years! The cripple was a burden until one day the burden-bearer stepped in, as Jesus stepped in the situation and the lame spirit stepped out. Isaiah 53:4 tells us that one of the names of Jesus Christ is burden bearer. At the name of Jesus this man became a marvel, a wonder. Everyone looked at him. "And said we know this man. He's been begging for alms for 40 years. How come he's now walking and leaping and praising God?" Have you been begging for clothes, have you been begging for contracts, have you been begging for job, and after getting the job you beg to stay employed. I prophesy, before the end of this year my God will pleasantly surprise you by lifting your burden in Jesus' name. Amen! Remain Blessed!

Prayer: *O Lord! Give me a pleasant surprise as You lift my burden, this day in Jesus' name. Amen!*

WORD SWORD OF THE ORACLE

The Word Today: Exodus 8:8 (NKJV)

*"Then Pharaoh called for Moses and Aaron, and said, "**Entreat** the Lord that He may take away the frogs from me and from my people; and I will let the people go, that they may sacrifice to the Lord."*

ENTREAT [HEBREW] *'ATAR*

*S*trong's concordance #6279 records the word *"Entreat"* in the Hebrew language [*'Atar*] as used in Ex. 8:8-9, Ex. 8:29-30, Ex. 9:28, Ex. 10:17-18. This term is translated *entreat* in Ex. 8:8 and *intercede* in Ex. 8:9 and it is one of many scriptural word used for prayer. The word portrays a person earnestly beseeching God; and it basically means "to ask." Gen. 25:21, Is. 19:22. In the Old Testament, spreading out your hands before God was a common gesture associated with prayer Ex. 9:29. This gesture expressed the petitioner's receptiveness to God, and his or her need or supplication and or petition. Empty-handedness, with nothing to offer but oneself, petitioner ask God to fill their hands with blessings. For this reason, God warned worshipers to petition Him with clean hands, with unsoiled hand and pure heart. Hand could be soiled by half heartedness in your offerings, Malachi 1:9 and insincerity of purpose.

There are two forms derived from this same verb. In 1611 KJV the spelling was indifferently "intreat" or "entreat." In 1760 editions of the King James Version "intreat" is used in the sense of "to beg"; "entreat" in the sense of "deal with." Here are some other examples and applications in the bible Ruth 1:16, 2 Corinthians 8:4, Genesis 25:21, Genesis 12:16, Acts 27:3, James 3:17, Job 19:17, Jeremiah 15:11, 1 Timothy 5:1, Philippians 4:3.

CHURCH AND HOME SUNDAY SCHOOL

WHAT IS A VOW?

A vow is a solemn promise made to God in which we dedicate ourselves to a certain act, service, or way of life. A marriage vow is an example.

"Yet *you ask, why does He reject it? Because the Lord was witness [to the covenant made at your marriage] between you and the wife of your youth, against whom you have dealt treacherously and to whom you were faithless. Yet she is your companion and the wife of your covenant [made by your marriage vows].* "Malachi 2:15 (AMP)

"*Moreover I call God as witness against my soul, that to spare you I came no more to Corinth.* "2 Corinthians 1:23 (NKJV)

WHEN DOES A VOW BECOME SINFUL?

A vow becomes sinful when it is taken falsely or carelessly.

"*Do not be hash with your mouth, and let not your heart utter anything hastily before God. For God is in heaven and you on earth; therefore let your words be few. For a dream comes through much activity. And a fool's voice is known by his many words. When you make a vow to God, do not delay to pay it; for He has no pleasure in fools. Pay what you have vowed. Better not to vow than to vow and not pay. Do not let your mouth cause your flesh to sin, nor say before the messenger of God that it was an error. Why should God be angry at your excuse[a] and destroy the work of your hands?*" Ecclesiastes 5:2-6 (NKJV)

BIBLE NARATIVES:

1. JEPHTHAH'S FOOLISH VOW: Judges 11:30

2. GOD IS AGAINST BROKEN MARRIAGE VOWS: Malachi 2:14-16

WHAT IS CURSING?

Cursing is the calling down of some evil on a person, self, place or on a thing. To wish someone bodily harm is against the love we owe our neighbors as instructed by God.

"With it we bless our God and Father, and with it we curse men, who have been made in the similitude of God. 10 Out of the same mouth proceed blessing and cursing. My brethren, these things ought not to be so." James 3:9-10 (NKJV)

SUNDAY SCHOOL QUESTIONS

Q1. WHAT IS A VOW?
Q2. WHEN DOES A VOW BECOME SINFUL?
Q3. WHAT IS CURSING?

> **Memory Verse:** "When you make a vow to God, do not delay to pay it; for He has no pleasure in fools. Pay what you have vowed. Better not to vow than to vow and not pay. Ecclesiastes 5:4

Today's Prayers

1. *Lord Forgive me of every broken vow that I have ever made!*
2. *Father! Give me the grace to fulfill my vows and pledge!*
3. *Lord Jesus! Grant me the grace to control my tongue!*
4. *I defy Satan's power upon my tongue, in Jesus' name.*
5. *Let water of life flush out every unwanted stranger in my life.*
6. *Thank God in advance for prayer answered!*

I PROPHESY! THE BLOCKADE TO MY BREAKTHROUGH IS LIFTED!

In Matthew 27:62-66, a day after the death and burial of Jesus Christ, the Pharisees and the Chief Priest who murdered Him came to Pontius Pilate to request permission to seal and guard His tomb properly; to ensure that Jesus did not rise as He said He would on the third day of His death. But they were mistaken! When God decides on a thing, no blockade or barrier can hinder or stop Him. The blockade at the sepulcher was so mighty that the women who wished to anoint the body of Jesus Christ could not move it, wondering, they said "who shall help us roll away the stone from the door of the sepulcher?" Mark 16:3. But little did they know that a surprise awaits them. I decree this day, a great surprise of breakthrough awaits you at your breaking point in the name of Jesus. Amen!

In verse 4 of Mark chapter 16, they saw that the stone was already rolled away, so they were able to enter into the tomb where they discovered that Jesus had risen. Saint, I don't know what is your own barrier in life. I may not know what blockade the enemy has put in place to hinder you from stepping into your divine destiny. They may have assigned a monitoring spirit or an agent of darkness to abort every of your effort to breakthrough. Whatever the case may be, I prophesy the hindrance in your life is hereby rolled away in the name of Jesus. Amen! The angel of the living God shall roll away every blockade to your testimony in the name of Jesus. Amen!

Prayer: *O Lord My God! Roll away every blockade to my breakthrough in Jesus' name. Amen!*

I PROFESS! I AM DIVINELY FAVORED!

*F*avor is most favorable in all constituents of success. Favor is the generous and unfair treatment you receive. Favor is a factor that ensures victory in all your endeavors. Favor is not the product of labor but the multiplication of the product of labor. When you are of God, it unleashes the grace of the LORD upon you. And this empowers you to overcome challenges of life with little or no effort on your part. Joseph's rise to prominence in Egypt was as a result of God's favor upon him. That is why, in spite of all the obstacles he encountered, treasures were entrusted into his hands. From Joseph' father's house; to Portiphar's house to prison and eventually to the palace in Egypt favor ensured that he was preferred above all others. No wonder, his story remains one of the greatest stories of divine promotion of all times. I prophesy this day; henceforth you are divinely favored in the name of Jesus. Amen!

Do you desire the manifestation of the above prophecy in your life? Then get a little anointing oil and smear on your fore head as you pray thus: *Lord Jesus! Forgive my all sins and have mercy upon me; Lord! Release Your grace for divine lifting into this oil right now in the name of Jesus. Lord as I anoint my head with this oil let the spirit of divine favor envelop me in the name of Jesus. Let Your favor that enabled Joseph to excel come upon me now in the name of Jesus Christ. Amen!*

As you follow the above instruction, I now join my faith with yours and declare upon you the anointing for divine favor!

I PROPHESY! IT IS MY TURN FOR DIVINE ELEVATION!

At various stages on his journey with Prophets Elijah, from Gilgal, through Bethel and to Jericho, the other sons of the prophet continued to mock Elisha. But because he was determined to receive a double portion of the anointing upon the life and ministry of Elijah, Elisha put up with all the abuse and slur.

Nevertheless, when the double portion anointing eventually rested upon him, and then parted River Jordan with the mantle of Elijah, the same sons of the prophets who jeered him, *"....came to meet him and bowed themselves to the ground before him."* 2 Kings 2:15.

Many people may have been ridiculing you because of your commitment and dedication to the things of the Kingdom of God. You may have been forsaken by the world due to one reproach or the other in your life. People might even be making fun of you because you have nothing to show for your hard work as of now. This day I stand as the Oracle of God, the mouthpiece of the LORD God of Elisha, the Most High and decree your divine elevation into manifestation in Jesus' name!

The same anointing that move Elisha from obscurity to prominence is hereby released upon you in the name of Jesus. Henceforth; as many as have ridiculed you, shall begin to reverence you. They will surely begin to treat you with utmost respect because God who changed the destiny of Elisha has this day spotlighted you for greatness in the mighty name of Jesus.

Prayer: *I am stepping out of obscurity this day in Jesus' name!*

The Word Today: Isaiah 65:24 (GWT)

"Before they call, I will answer. While they're still speaking, I will hear."

THE LORD GOD SHALL TREAT MY ISSUES WITH URGENCY!

A famed minister of the gospel once told a story that fittingly depicts the above prophecy. *"According to him, he was traveling with some foreign guest in an airplane when suddenly the aircraft began to experiencing technical difficulties. After trying all in their power, the technical crew resigned to fate and expected the worst. Scared to death his guest turned to him for comfort. Then he knelt down, looked up to heaven and cried unto God in a loud voice, to treat the situation as an emergency by intervening immediately. And God intervened instantly; as the situation returned to normalcy and the aircraft landed smoothly."* Glory to God!

There are situations that require instant divine intervention. There are emergency situations like a woman who is unmarried at the age of forty-five, a graduate of many years without a job, a couple who have been married for over ten years without a child or someone facing deportation etc.; are you in some emergency situations. Peradventure, you are passing through any of these situations; I prophesy that respite will come your way now because heaven shall treat your case as an emergency in Jesus' name. Be expectant, for my God shall intervene on your behalf today in Jesus' name. Amen!

Prayer: *My Lord and My God, I call upon you now, intervene in my situation **(State your specific problem)** and let it be resolved within the next seven days in Jesus' name. Amen!*

September 19th

The Word Today: Matthew 22:12-13

"... "Friend, how did you come in here without a wedding garment?" And he was speechless. Then the king said to the servants, "Bind him hand and foot, take him away, and cast him into outer darkness; there will be weeping and gnashing of teeth."

LORD JESUS! MAKE ME READY NOW!

We all have such a very short time to get ready for such a very long time of eternity. We have but only now to prepare for then that is to come. We have this very moment to prepare for "ZILLIONS" of years in eternity. To fail to get ready is an act of decent foolishness indeed. I like you to know that we all, have been given time to be ready for eternity; it is an act of inexcusable recklessness to let anything hinder your readiness. If you find yourselves in a spiritual pothole, nothing in the world should hinder you now. Nothing in this world is worth it. If you believe in eternity, if you believe in God, if you believe in the eternal existence of life after death then there is nothing more important to cause you to commit such an act of moral folly of unpreparedness. Failing to be ready now for eternity, is a trap in plain sight. There is an odd saying in Proverbs 1:17 it says *"How useless to spread a net in full view of all the birds".* When the man of God wrote that, he gave the birds a little credit. It would be silly for a bird watching us set the trap to conveniently fly down and get into it. Yet we are doing that all the time. We, who have to live for eternity fall into that trap set for us in plain sight by the devil. Pray thus:

Prayer: *"Lord! Enable me to prepare for eternity. Give me the willingness and passion to do my part now in Jesus' name!*

102

September 20th

WORD SWORD OF THE ORACLE

The Word Today: Exodus 15:13 (NKJV)

"You in Your mercy have led forth the people whom You have **redeemed;** *You have guided them in Your strength to Your holy habitation."*

REDEEMED [HEBREW] *GA'AL*

𝒯he word redeemed which is *[Ga'al]* in Hebrew as use in Exodus 15:13, Ruth 4:4, Isaiah 43:14 Strong's concordance #1350. Has the basic meaning of "redeem", "to deliver", "to rescue", "to protect family rights of close relatives." To buy back family estate and persons that has been sold due to debts." Leviticus 25:25-26.

The same Hebrew word is used to describe Boaz's kindness to Ruth. Boaz not only bought back the family land, but also saved Ruth from poverty Ruth 4:3-11. Boaz's kindness and willingness to save Ruth is a picture of the kindness of God. The Israelites had become the family of God Ex. 4:22, Ex. 13:2. God had freely taken on the responsibility to buy them back, to pay the price to free them from poverty and slavery. The LORD was Israel's Redeemer as Isaiah proclaimed in the book of Isaiah 43:14.

God was also the personal Redeemer of both Job; Job 19:25 and David Psalm 19:14. We too have a Redeemer Jesus Christ, who is willing to pay the price, and did with His blood, by His own death on the cross of Calvary to free us from our sins. Galatians 4:5, and from the curse of the law Galatians 3:13-14, Titus 2:14. Glory be to God.

Prayer: *Lord! I thank You for sending Your Son to redeem me!*
103

CHURCH AND HOME SUNDAY SCHOOL

WHAT IS BLASPHEMY?

Blasphemy is insulting language which expressed contempt for God. When a knowledgeable person willfully attributes to the devil those works which could only be wrought by God, this is blasphemy against the Holy Spirit. Blasphemy against the Holy Spirit is the unpardonable sin.

"Assuredly, I say to you, all sins will be forgiven the sons of men, and whatever blasphemies they may utter; but he who blasphemes against the Holy Spirit never has forgiveness, but is subject to eternal condemnation" because they said, "He has an unclean spirit." Mark 3:28-30 (NKJV)

BIBLE NARRATIVES:

1. THE JEWS REVILED JESUS CHRIST WHEN HE WAS HANGED ON THE CROSS: Matthew 27:27-43
2. RABSHAKEH BLASPHEMED THE GOD OF ISRAEL 2 Kings 18:25-37; 2 Kings 19:21-22

WHAT IS USING WITCHCRAFT BY GOD'S NAME?

It is using God's name in order to perform some supernatural act with the help of the devil; for example, conjuring magic, sorcery, etc.; fortunetelling or consulting the dead and horoscope.

"There shall not be found among you anyone who makes his son or his daughter pass through the fire, or one who practices witchcraft, or a soothsayer, or one who interprets omens, or a sorcerer, or one who conjures spells, or a medium, or a spiritist, or one who calls up the dead. For all who do these things are an abomination to the Lord, and because of these abominations the Lord your God drives them out from before you." Deuteronomy 18:10-12 (NKJV)

WHAT IS LYING AND DECEIVING BY GOD'S NAME? IT IS:

1. Teaching false doctrine and saying that it is God's word or revelation.
2. False prophecies, prophesying and giving a message in the unknown tongue with an interpretation without the anointing enabling power of the Holy Spirit.
3. Hypocrisy: Covering up an unbelieving heart or a sinful life by a show of piety.

"Behold, I am against the prophets, says the Lord, who use their [own deceitful] tongues and say, Thus says the Lord. Behold, I am against those who prophesy lying dreams, says the Lord, and tell them and cause My people to err and go astray by their lies and by their vain boasting and recklessness—when I did not send them or command them; nor do they profit these people at all, says the Lord." Jeremiah 23:31-32 (AMP)

"Whatever I command you, be careful to observe it; you shall not add to it nor take away from it." Deuteronomy 12:32 (NKJV)

HOW CAN WE BEST KEEP THE THIRD COMMANDMENT?

By, calling upon God's name in every need and deed; in praying, fasting, praising and thanksgiving.

SUNDAY SCHOOL QUESTIONS

Q1. WHAT IS BLASPHEMY?
Q2. WHAT IS USING WITCHCRAFT BY GOD'S NAME?
Q3. WHAT IS LYING AND DECEIVING BY GOD'S NAME?

Q4. HOW CAN WE BEST KEEP THE THIRD COMMANDMENT?

Today's Memory Verse:
"Whatever I command you, be careful to observe it; you shall not add to it nor take away from it." Deuteronomy 12:32 (NKJV)

Today's Prayers

1. Lord! Forgive me of any conscious or unconscious sin of blasphemy in the name of Jesus!
2. I frustrate every witchcraft arrest over my spirit-man.
3. Father! Deliver me from lying tongue in Jesus' name!
4. Let the blood of Jesus remove any unprogressive label from every aspect of my life, in Jesus' name.
5. Anti-breakthrough decrees, be revoked, in Jesus' name.
6. Holy Ghost fire, destroy every satanic garments in my life.
7. I refuse to disobey the voice of God, in the name of Jesus.
8. Every root of rebellion in my life, be uprooted, in Jesus' name.
9. Fountain of rebellion in my life, dry up, in Jesus' name.
10. Contrary powers fueling rebellion in my life, die by fire.
11. Every inspiration of witchcraft in my family, be destroyed now.
12. Blood of Jesus, blot out every evil mark of witchcraft in me.
13. Every garment put upon me by witchcraft, be torn to pieces.
14. Angels of God, begin to pursue my household enemies, let their ways be dark and slippery, in the name of Jesus.

I AM MOVING FROM A VICTIM TO A VICTOR!

The Philistines had always being arch-enemies of Israel. They had a highly skilled army, which took Israel to task many times in the Scriptures. Severally, they held Israel in bondage and tormented them. Whenever such occasions arose, they never lost the opportunity to make Israel suffer. That was the situation in 1 Samuel 7.

As soon as they learnt that the Israelites were gathered at a particular location; Mizpeh, they besieged them. That action sent panic and fear upon the Israelites. So, they were victims of the Philistine strength. But as soon as Samuel shed the innocent blood of the lamb, God arose against the Army of the Philistine and discomfited them. Consequently, within a short while, the Israelites who were hitherto victims now became victors over the Philistines.

Saint, if there is a force of adversity that has made your life tortuous, up till now; the Lord will bulldoze them in Jesus' name. It does not matter how long it has been in your bloodline. Today, by the power in the blood of Jesus, I prophesy, you shall move from victim to victor in the name of Jesus. That age old struggle is over because the Lord will discomfit your enemies in Jesus' name. Amen!

Prayer: *"Henceforth, I shall no longer be a victim. I am now a victor. No power can hold me hostage in Jesus' name. Amen!"*

September 23rd

The Word Today: 2 Samuel 9:1-7

I PROPHESY! GOD WILL REMEMBER ME FOR LIFTING!

Is it not strange how certain events happen? Many people lived and worked in the palace with King David. Some would have been praying and clamoring for promotion. Several others may have done several things to seek and attract the favor of the king. But that morning David did not choose to promote any of them. Instead, he asked for Mephibosheth, a man whom he had never encountered, the grandson of David's arch-enemy, Saul.

Saint I prophesy! This season God will show you His mercy and favor and you will enjoy His goodness in the name of Jesus Christ. It does not take God forever to bless a person of interest. Like He chose to use David to lift Mephibosheth instantly, it takes God just an instant to lift a downtrodden person to an exalted place. The day before Mephibosheth was remembered, he lived in abject poverty. But after he received the king's favor, he became a man of great substance in the midst of royalty. I prophesy to you now, God has decided to lift you and your loved ones out of your misery this day in the name of Jesus. The Lord wants you to begin to rejoice and be filled with the joy of salvation for deliverance cometh to you speedily this day. Sing praises to the almighty God now because the second half of this year will bring you unexpected breakthroughs in the name of Jesus. Amen! According to our text-verses above, you have been mark for goodness and kindness by the Lord God Almighty. You are coming out of Lodebar for there is vacancy for you at the top in Jesus' mighty name. Amen!

Prayer: *Lord! Remember me for mercy and favor in Jesus' name.*

GOD WILL GIVE ME HIDDEN RICHES OF SECRET PLACES!

In his masterpiece "Acres of Diamond" Dr. Russell Conwell wrote about a man called Al-Hafid who sold his estate for a meager sum and went to a distant land in search of diamonds. Few weeks after, he died in the strange land; the person who bought his previous estate accidently discovered diamonds in the compound of Al-Hafid. The estate which covers several acres was discovered to be a mine full of diamonds. So, all the while before he sold off his estate and went off in search of diamonds, Al-Hafid had lived on top of acres of diamond without knowing it. That is because, for Al-Hafid, the diamonds were hidden riches of secret place. Dr. Conwell's masterpiece figuratively describes the lives of many today. People erroneously believe that the wealth they desire is in a different location from where they are. Whereas some think their breakthrough is in other countries, others believe that theirs are in a different state, city or vocation. That is a vagabond spirit.

The truth is that, it is possible to be wealthy right where you are. The only essential to that is for God to reveal the secret of breakthrough to you. If you understand this principle, apply and pray it through, you would become wealthy. Whatsoever is it you do or desire to do? If you can find a better way of improving on your efficiency and reduce cost you will become wealthy. You can even become wealthier if you sell that idea; that is working for you to others. Your task is to pray that God reveals unto you secrets and wisdom to success. God bless you!

Prayer: *O God, open my eyes to see opportunities around me!*

THE DOOR OF MY BREAKTHROUGH IS NOW WIDE OPEN!

*A*nnually, during the dispensation of the Law of Moses; the High Priest would slay a goat or lamb and sprinkle its blood on the altar and the mercy seat as atonement for the sin of the people of Israel to access God's Holy place, the Holy of Holies.

This was the case until the atoning death of Jesus Christ on Mount Calvary; the veil barring entrance into the Holy places of the temple instantly was torn from top to bottom Mark 15:38. By implication, the blood of Jesus made atonement for mankind, and terminated the dispensation of the Law of Moses, thus making it possible for everyone to access God by faith in Jesus Christ, everyone who comes to Him by faith in the finished work of Christ Jesus on Calvary.

At Calvary, Christ opened unto us the doors of the blessings of heaven. Therefore, there is no legal ground whatsoever for you to be bound by poverty, sickness, diseases, afflictions etc. Nevertheless, if you are bound by any afflictions or infirmities, today I invoke the power in that shed blood of Jesus and decree that every chain and padlock holding you down is broken now in the name of Jesus. And the doors of all your held-down blessings are hereby released in the name of Jesus. Receive now your breakthrough as you believe in Jesus' mighty name. Amen! Glory to God!

Prayer: *Every door that is holding down my blessing, I command you open now in the name of Jesus Christ. Amen!*

September 26th

The Word Today: 2 Kings 6:1-7 (ASV)

"... he cut down a stick, and cast it in thither, and made the iron to swim. And he said, Take it up to thee. So he put out his hand, and took it."

I PROPHESY! I SHALL RECOVER MY LOST STRENGHT!

When the enemy wants to stall your progress, he attacks and steals your strength. That is what he did to the sons of the prophets in 2 Kings 6. The sons of the prophets were tired of stagnation. They desired to make progress by expanding their habitation. To execute their scheme, they borrowed an axe to cut wood beams they needed for their construction task.

That axe was the most effective weapon they had. Their only hope of ever completing the project was largely dependent on that axe. In fact that axe represented their strength. So, as soon as the axe head fell into the water, their progress was effectively stalled. But when they called to Prophet Elisha for help, the Oracle of God mobilized the forces of heaven to make an axe head, a heavy metal with high density to float, defying the law of gravity.

Saint, have you lost a particular source of strength? Have you lost a high paying job you once had? It may be a sponsor who died. It may even be a lost business opportunity. Whatsoever it is that you have lost, I prophesy a recovery of your lost strength now in Jesus' name! However, like the sons of the prophet, you have to stretch your hand to pick it up 2 Kings 6:7. Therefore, arise and step into your breakthrough in Jesus' name. Amen!

Prayer: *I command a restoration of all my lost glory and strength in Jesus' name. Amen!"*

WORD SWORD OF THE ORACLE

The Word Today: Exodus 3:8

---

*"So I have come down to **deliver** them out of the hand of the Egyptians, and to bring them up from that land to a good and large land, to a land flowing with milk and honey, to the place of the Canaanites and the Hittites and the Amorites and the Perizzites and the Hivites and the Jebusites.*

DELIVERED [HEBREW] *NATSAL*

In Strong's #5337 is the Hebrew word *[Natsal] as used in* Exodus 3:8, Judges 6:9, 1 Samuel 10:18. This Hebrew verb may either mean 'to strip, to plunder' or 'to snatch away, to deliver.' The word is often used to describe God's work in delivering or rescuing the Israelite from slavery. Exodus 3:8, Exodus 6:6.

The term sometimes signifies God's deliverance of His people from sin and guilt. Psalm 51:14. The word is a statement of God's supremacy over the Egyptian pantheon of deities. The LORD was so powerful that He could "snatch the entire nation of Israel from Pharaoh's grasp Exodus 18:10. This was only the beginning, for God repeatedly delivered the Israelites from their enemies. Joshua 11:6, Judges 3:9. God was their Deliverer, and the Psalmists proclaim this fact with Joy in Psalm 18:12 (NKJV) *"From the brightness before Him, His thick clouds passed with hailstones and coals of fire."*

And in Psalm 144:2 (NKJV) *"My lovingkindness and My fortress, My high tower and My deliverer, My shield and the One in Whom I take refuge, Who subdues my people under me.*

Prayer: *Father! Deliver me from the Pharaoh of my destiny!*

CHURCH AND HOME SUNDAY SCHOOL

THE FOURTH CONMMANDMENT

WHAT IS THE FOURTH COMMANDMENT?

"Remember the Sabbath day, to keep it holy." Exodus 20:8

WHAT IS THE SABBATH DAY?

The Sabbath Day is the seventh day, Saturday. The Hebrew word Sabbath means rest. God rested and hallowed the seventh day. By the law given at Sinai, the seventh day was to be a day of rest in which no secular work was to be done and which was to be kept holy unto God.

HOW DID JESUS OBSERVE THE SABBATH?

Jesus Christ fulfilled the Sabbath law by completely ceasing from His own labors and resting absolutely in God's will. By performing God's will and purposes on earth and permitting the Holy Spirit to direct Him, Jesus became the Master or the Lord of the Sabbath. *"For the Son of Man is Lord even of the Sabbath."* Matthew 12:8 (NKJV)

ARE CHRISTIANS REQUIRED TO OBSERVE THE SABBATH AND OTHER HOLY DAYS?

No! The Sabbath and many of the Jewish holy days were given their true meaning in Jesus Christ. When we come to God through the redemption provided by Jesus Christ, the redemptive price which the precious blood of Jesus; has already been paid for our souls. There is nothing more we can do to make ourselves more acceptable to God. We can now rest from our own labors. Jesus Christ is our Sabbath. When we accept Him as our salvation, we cease from our works and rest in His grace. The Sabbath now is no longer a day, but a spiritual experience. *"Come to Me, all you who labor and are heavy laden, and I will give you rest."* Matthew 11:28 (NKJV)

"For it is by free grace (God's unmerited favor) that you are saved and delivered from judgment and made partakers of Christ's salvation) through [your] faith. And this [salvation] is not of yourselves [of your own doing, it came not through your own striving], but it is the gift of God; Not because of works [not the fulfillment of the Law's demands], lest any man should boast. It is not the result of what anyone can possibly do, so no one can pride himself in it or take glory to himself." Ephesians 2:8-9

"Therefore let no one sit in judgment on you in matters of food and drink, or with regard to a feast day or a New Moon or a Sabbath. Such [things] are only the shadow of things that are to come, and they have only a symbolic value. But the reality (the substance, the solid fact of what is foreshadowed, the body of it) belongs to Christ." Colossians 2:16-18 (AMP)

SUNDAY SCHOOL QUESTIONS

Q1. WHAT IS THE FOURTH COMMANDMENT?
Q2. WHAT IS THE SABBATH DAY?
Q3. HOW DID JESUS OBSERVE THE SABBATH?
Q4. ARE CHRISTIANS REQUIRED TO OBSERVE THE SABBATH AND OTHER HILY DAYS?

Memory Verse: Matthew 12:8 (NKJV) *"For the Son of Man is Lord even of the Sabbath."*

Today's Prayers: *Take religion and tradition from heart so that I can worship you in spirit and in truth in Jesus' name!*

114

I WILL SURELY OVERCOME IN JESUS' NAME!

*A*re you faced up with obstacles on the way to your breakthrough? Are you in the middle of a life test? Have satanic agents conspired to pull you down with their evil plots? Saint, fear not, for I have good news for you this day. As long as you focus on Jesus Christ, you will surely over come in the name of Jesus! The tests and trials you are going through, that seem like obstacles, are actually gateways to your miracles. They are God permitted hindrances to ascertain your qualification for a greater position. From time past; it had been declared that Jesus was the son of God. Even during His baptism, the voice of God from heaven confirmed it. Nevertheless, He did not assume His high office until after several temptations and tests that led even unto His death.

Matthew 4:17 *"from that time Jesus began to preach and to say, repent for the kingdom of God is at hand"*. By inference, until He crossed the hurdles of the trials and temptations of the devil, Jesus was not qualified to assume the fullness of His calling. So also it is in our Christian walk today. Whether or not a student moves to the next higher grade or class is determined by his or her performance at the end of semester examinations. Are you facing difficulties in life? I admonish you to confront that situation with the right mindset. Know that at the end lies a great opportunity for self improvement. Focus on Jesus Christ to see you through and you will overcome in His name!

Prayer: *I receive the grace to overcome my trials and tribulations in Jesus' name. Amen!*

The Word Today: Luke 23:34

"Then Jesus said, "Father, forgive them, for they do not know what they do. And they divided His garments and cast lots."

THE LORD GOD SHALL GIVE ME THE GRACE TO FORGIVE OTHERS!

*O*ne truth every believer should know is that forgiveness is the path to greatness and lavish blessings. It is a higher law that is always applied by great minds of all ages to access God's Blessing. Brethren, I want you to know that your passport to greater glory is to forgive unconditionally. When people refuse to forgive others, they do so at their own peril. Un-forgiveness is a barrier to breakthrough. It is such a formidable barrier that Jesus advised those who seek divine intervention to be sure to forgive all that has offended them.

Many times I have handled situations where people's prayers are not answered until they forgave those who had offended them. So, I can authoritatively affirm that un-forgiveness is a major blockade to miracles. Joseph knew this principle. That is why he did not harbor any grudge against his brothers for selling him into slavery Genesis 45. Instead, he applied the principle that is above all; love. He conquered their hatred with love and stepped into the realm of supernatural abundance. Are you one of those that find it almost impossible to forgive? If you are, please ask God in prayer to give you the grace and capacity to forgive all those that have trespassed against you now so that you too can be forgiven your trespasses.

Prayer: *Oh Lord My God! Give me a heart to forgive those who offend me and help me move ahead with my life in Jesus' name!*

I RECEIVE THE GRACE TO GLORIFY GOD IN ALL THINGS!

$\mathcal{Y}$ou know you can pray enough but you can never praise God enough. You can pray amiss but you can never praise amiss. It is possible to wake up in the morning and be dead before the day ends. When God says 'time up' it's time up. So the fact that you are alive today is simply by His grace. You are not better or smarter than any of the people who are dead. So more than anything else, you need to praise Him now. I want you to humble yourself before the Almighty God, just praise Him.

PRAYER OF PRAISE AND THANKS:

Eternal Rock of Ages, the Alpha, the Omega, the Beginning, the Ending, the Unchangeable Lord, the Holy one of Israel, the Lion of the tribe of Judah, the Bright and Morning Star, I bless your holy name. You are greater than the greatest, better than the best, older than the oldest, wiser than the wisest, better than the best, stronger than the strongest, glory be to your holy name. Accept my worship in Jesus' name. Amen!

OCTOBER BIRTHDAY AND WEDDING ANNIVERSARY PRAYERS!

October is the tenth months of the year; ten is five times two, and five is the number grace, undeserved favor. So, ten is the number for double grace. Father, I thank You for Your children born in October and those wedded and wedding this month, thank You for preserving their lives, Father, release on them double grace, in all areas of their lives, let their blessings be doubled in Jesus' gracious name. Amen!

MY BLESSINGS SHALL BE TRANSFERRED TO MY CHILDREN!

*M*any men and women, in their lifetime lived in opulence but their children are suffering generationally. In some cases, the level of hardship experienced by these children lends credence to the supposition that their progenitors usurped their blessings. Such blessings did not have its source from God because the blessings of the Lord maketh rich and add no sorrows with it. The generational blessings of Abraham, Isaac and Jacob etc., was overflowing blessings; that ensured that they enjoyed opulence in their lifetime and transferred great wealth and affluence unto their children and future generations; I pray that such blessings shall be your portion in the name of Jesus. Amen! Abraham became a beneficiary of that blessing because of his obedience to God. That was so important to God that the lifetime of Abraham was not enough to carry the reward of his obedience to God, so the LORD God had to transfer the blessings to the children. Do you desire that kind of blessings? All you have to do is to study and obey the word of God. When you live in obedience to God's word, your life would definitely become a carrier of generational blessings which would be passed onto your children generationally. This day by the power of the Holy Spirit, I release that grace of God upon you in the name of Jesus. Henceforth, you are a candidate of God's generational blessings. All you have to do now is to serve God with all your heart and might. As you do so, you will be so blessed that your blessings shall be transferred unto your children in Jesus' name. Amen!

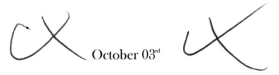

October 03rd

The Word Today: Exodus 14:21-28

THE LORD SHALL BURY ALL MY STUBBORN PURSUERS!

After God sent the angel of death to slay the first born of Egypt, Pharaoh was quick to set the children of Israel free from slavery. Exodus 12:29-37. However, as soon as they departed, Pharaoh and his host pursued to destroy them. Soon, the Israelites came to the red sea. And God through Moses parted the sea to see them through.

Considering his ordeal with the ten plagues, one would expect Pharaoh to have stopped the pursuit for fear of the almighty God of Israel. But never! He continued because he was a very stubborn enemy. He did not stop until he was buried with his host in the watery grave of the Red Sea. I see all your stubborn pursuers buried this day in the name of Jesus. Amen!

Pharaoh and his army may be history, but such stubborn adversaries still exist today. They may have been pursuing and persecuting you and your loved ones even before your birth. They refused to allow you to be what you are destined to be. Such problems, their causes and sources will have to give way for your life to have any meaning. This day as the Oracle of the Most High God, I prophesy every stubborn pursuer of your destiny is buried alive in the belly of the Red Sea in the name of Jesus. Amen! As you receive, believe and claim this word of prophecy, those forces around you will collapse and will never rise again in Jesus' mighty name. Amen!

Prayer: *Every Stubborn adversary in my life I command you drown and be buried alive in the name of Jesus. Amen!*

119

October 04th

WORD SWORD OF THE ORACLE

The Word Today: Exodus 13:2 (NKJV)

*"**Consecrate** to Me all the firstborn, whatever opens the womb among the children of Israel, both of man and beast; it is Mine."*

CONSECRATE [HEBREW] *QUADASH*

In the Bible the word consecration means "the separation of oneself from things that are unclean, especially anything that would contaminate one's relationship with a perfect God." Consecration also carries the connotation of sanctification, holiness, or purity.

Strong's #6942 translates the Hebrew word [QUADASH] as consecrate as used in Exodus 13:2, Exodus 19:10, Exodus 29:44. This Hebrew verb means "To Make Holy" "To Declare Distinct" or "To Set Apart." The word describes dedicating an object or person to God. By delivering the Children of Israel from slavery in Egypt, God made the nation of Israel distinct. Through His mighty acts of deliverance, God demonstrated that the Israelites were His people, and He was their God Exodus 6:7. By having the people wash themselves at Mount Sinai, the LORD made it clear that they, as a people were being set apart for Him Exodus 19:10. Just like the Israelites, Christians also have been delivered, from slavery to sin. The deliverance has set us apart. We have been dedicated to our Savior and His purpose. We have been called to be His holy people 1 Peter 1:15-16, 1 Peter 2:9-10. **Here are some other related scriptures about consecration:** Joshua 3:5, 1 Corinthians 7:1-6, Psalm 51:2, Psalm 51:7, Psalm 77:13-14, 2 Samuel 12:20, Colossians 3:5-14; Ephesians 4:26-27, 2 Corinthians 6:17, Romans 12:1-2.

1ˢ Sunday of the Month of October

CHURCH AND HOME SUNDAY SCHOOL

WHY IS THE SABBATH REFFERED TO AS A SHADOW OF THE THINGS TO COME?

*B*ecause it encourages us to enter into the Sabbath rest by resting in the Spirit of God within us, as He directs us in performing the will of God on earth.

"For what the law could not do in that it was weak through the flesh, God did by sending His own Son in the likeness of sinful flesh, on account of sin: He condemned sin in the flesh, that the righteous requirement of the law might be fulfilled in us who do not walk according to the flesh but according to the Spirit." Romans 8:3-4 (NKJV)

"There remains therefore a rest for the people of God. For he who has entered His rest has himself also ceased from his works as God did from His." Hebrews 4:9-10 (NKJV)

DID GOD COMMAND CHRISTIANS TO OBSERVE ANY DAY?

No! Christians are not commanded to observe any day.

"One person esteems one day above another; another esteems every day alike. Let each be fully convinced in his own mind. He who observes the day, observes it to the Lord; and he who does not observe the day, to the Lord he does not observe it. He who eats, eats to the Lord, for he gives God thanks; and he who does not eat, to the Lord he does not eat, and gives God thanks." Romans 14:5-6 (NKJV)

"You observe days and months and seasons and years. I am afraid for you, lest I have labored for you in vain." Galatians 4:10-11 (NKJV)

DO WE OBSERVE SUNDAY AND OTHER CHURCH FESTIVITIES DAYS AS HOLY DAYS?

No! We observe these days in other to have time and opportunity for public worship and fellowship.

"Not forsaking or neglecting to assemble together [as believers], as is the habit of some people, but admonishing (warning, urging, and encouraging) one another, and all the more faithfully as you see the day approaching." Hebrews 10:25 (AMP)

"And they steadfastly persevered, devoting themselves constantly to the instruction and fellowship of the apostles, to the breaking of bread [including the Lord's Supper] and prayers." Acts 2:42 (AMP)

SUNDAY SCHOOL QUESTIONS

Q1. WHY IS THE SABBATH REFFERED TO AS A SHADOW OF THE THINGS TO COME?
Q2. DID GOD COMMAND CHRISTIANS TO OBSERVE ANY DAY?   Q3. DO WE OBSERVE SUNDAY AND OTHER CHURCH FESTIVITIES DAYS AS HOLY DAYS?

Today's Memory Verse:
"For he who has entered His rest has himself also ceased from his works as God did from His." Hebrews 4:10 (NKJV)

Prayer: *Lord Jesus! Give me the grace to enter into Your rest in the gracious name of Jesus*

October 06th

The Word Today: Revelation 12:11

"And they overcame him by the blood of the Lamb and by the word of their testimony; and they loved not their lives unto the death."

I SHALL OVERCOME MY ENEMIES BY MY TESTIMONIES!

In 1 Samuel 17:36-37 *"David said unto Saul... thy servant slew both the lion and the bear; and this uncircumcised Philistine..."* Proverbs 18:21 says *"Death and life are in the power of the tongue...."*

David surely understood that statement. That is why he made the battle with Goliath a battle of testimonies. Even when the giant tried to run him down psychologically by boasting that he would give his flesh to the birds of the air, David countered that declaration with the name of God in 1 Samuel 17:44-45. No wonder, he defeated Goliath, a man that sent shivers down the spine of King Saul.

Like David, you can overcome your problems with the words of your testimony today. Has God done anything for you before? Has He delivered you from sickness, poverty, and death etc., in the past? If so, He can also deliver you now. So, whatsoever you are going through right now has a solution in what you speak. Begin to declare the testimonies of those things God has previously done for you against the situation you are facing now. As you do, your problems would melt away like wax on fire in the name of Jesus. I prophesy you shall overcome your enemies by the words of your testimony in Jesus' name. Amen!

Prayer: *Lord! Every problem I am facing is temporary and will become a testimony speedily in the name of Jesus. Amen!*

LESSONS FROM MARK 11:1-10 PART ONE

MY SITUATION NOW, WILL NOT DETERMINE MY FUTURE!

Our text-passage above is a very popular scripture. Jesus sent His disciple up front to a village ahead. He said as you enter, you will find a donkey tied at a junction, which no man has ever ridden on. He said lose it and bring it and if anyone asked you why you are losing the colt tell them the Lord has need for it. And so they went, loosed the donkey, brought it to Jesus and Jesus rode the colt to Jerusalem as the celebration began. People strewed their cloths together and laid them on the road for the colt to ride on. Others cut down palm trees [the reason for Palm Sunday] and they were shouting Hosanna, Hosanna blessed is He that cometh in the name of the Lord. Alleluia!

This passage as it is: is loaded with a lot of messages and lessons. Lesson one: It tells us that our present situation does not determine our future. No one knew that donkey, nobody has previously ridden on the donkey, here was a donkey that was destined to carry the King of glory, the King of kings and the Lord of lords but tied down somewhere in a obscure village doing nothing. The donkey did not know that a day will come where everybody would be reading about him like you are doing today. It didn't know it will be in the book of life. The fact that the donkey was tied down did not determine his future. So I prophesy your present situation will not determine your future!

Prayer: *Lord Jesus! By Your Fire power! My present situation will not determine my future condition in Jesus' name. Amen!*

LESSONS FROM MARK 11:1-10 PART TWO

MY PRESENT CRISIS DOESN'T SPELL FUTURE CALAMITY

The second lesson in the above scripture for us is that; our present crises, the crises we have being dealing with does not mean future hopelessness. A lot of people are going through terrible situations, in their marriages, finances, Job, business, education, health and career etc., and these situations are causing people to almost lose their minds. They don't even know what the future holds for them and their loved ones. I come to declare to you this day, that your present situation does not mean that your future is hopeless in the name of Jesus.

Is your life situation like the sad story of the donkey in our text-passage? Are you hopeless in your marriage? Is it in your finances, Job, business, education, health and career etc.? I have great news for you this day; you are coming out of that state of hopelessness in the gracious name of Jesus Christ. The donkey was tied down. It could not go anywhere it wants to go; the donkey was limited to the length of the evil cord that held it to the post; going round and round in a vicious circle. That was serious bondage, but that bondage did not make its future hopeless. I speak to your spirit man now; you are coming out of whatever bondage of hopelessness you are in; in the name of Jesus. Amen!

Prayer:

Lord Jesus! Get me out of the valley of hopelessness in the name of Jesus. Amen!

125

October 09th

The Word Today: Mark 11:1-10

LESSONS FROM MARK 11:1-10 PART THREE

MY URGLY SITUATION SHALL NOT DETERMINE MY FUTURE!

The third lesson from our working scripture is that, the ugly situation confronting you now does not say all about your future. Your present situation does not say everything about your future. The passage is saying whatever crises you are passing through now, are just a comma, not a period or a full stop. Your issue right now is just a pause but not a stop. And very soon the master of all situations Jesus Christ shall come to your aid and rescue you. The Psalmist says my help comes from the Lord who made the heavens and the earth.

That chain does not mean there is no hope for your future. The chain of embarrassment did not dictate the future of the colt. I am praying for you now, whatever stage you are now, whatever step you are taking now will be a stepping stone to your promotion in the name of Jesus. Amen! Psalm 23:5 *says "thou prepare a table before me in the presence of my enemy."* This is your portion in the name of Jesus. Amen!

Pray the following prayers:

1. I decree and declare those who are laughing at me now; they shall witness my testimonies and begin to laugh with me!

2. My test will become my testimonies in Jesus' name!
3. My trial and tribulation will become my triumph!
4. My break downs will become breakthroughs in Jesus' name.
5. My setback is a set up for my comeback in Jesus' name!

LESSONS FROM MARK 11:1-11 PART FOUR

I PROPHESY I SHALL FULFILL MY DIVINE DESTINY!

*M*any are actually destined for greatness but are limited right now like the donkey in Mark 11:1-11. They are just surviving; you hear them say it is the survival of the fittest. I say to you this day, no more survival; you will begin to experience the Lord's revival in every aspect of your life in Jesus' name. Amen! If God will open your eyes to see what you ought to be, when I say pray for one hour, you would pray for nine hours. I tell you it is possible for you to be dreaming dreams of great heights to which the almighty is calling you. But yet all your experience in real life is chains and shackles of hindrances.

Saint, the final verdict for your future does not depend on those chains you are in right now, but lies with our Lord Jesus Christ. He who planned greatness for you is stronger than the chains placed upon you. *The chains shall be broken and your enemies shall be disgraced in Jesus' name. Amen!* God is stronger than all the witches and wizards, witch doctors and voodoo priest standing by saying let us see who would break this chain off him.

I PRAYER FOR YOU NOW!

1. You have being struggling for too long but this day God is taking the struggles out of your life in the name of Jesus!
2. You have been placed in categories but I come to de-categorize you this day in the name of Jesus.
3. You have being limited for too long, the Lord sent me to come and decree your de-limitation in the name of Jesus. Amen!

October 11th

WORD SWORD OF THE ORACLE

The Word Today: Exodus 23:17

---

*"Three times in the year all your males shall appear before the **Lord God**."*

THE LORD GOD [HEBREW- *YHWH*] *ADONAI*

In Strong's #113 and #3068 is the Hebrew word [Adonai] which means The Lord God. This is a rare description of God linking God with the title *Adonai* meaning 'Lord' or 'Master.' Adonai is a plural composite of Adon + "ai" literally translated "My Lord" or "Lord" (capital "L" followed by small letters. In contrast with Jehovah which is rendered in all caps [LORD] in NAS, ESV, KJV).

Adonai is said to be a plural of majesty like Elohim and these plural form of both names of God also points to the truth of the Trinity in the Old Testament

Adonai is linked with God's personal name YHWH pronounced Yahweh. The title speaks of God's unlimited power and authority [Omnipotence] just as a master had unlimited power over a slave or servant. On the other hand, God's personal name Yahweh invokes His unlimited mercifulness, His unlimited faithfulness and His unlimited righteous character. Yahweh is spelled with four consonants in Hebrew. YHWH!

The Jews do not pronounce this sacred name of God and instead read Adonai wherever the name occurs in the Scriptures. Its precise meaning and pronunciation is unknown. Most probably the name Yahweh [YHWH] is derived from the Hebrew verb "to be" meaning "I AM WHO I AM" Exodus 3:14.

Prayer: *O Lord My God! Be my Adonai in Jesus' name!*

2ⁿᵈ Sunday of the Month of October

CHURCH AND HOME SUNDAY SCHOOL

WHY DO WE WORSHIP TOGETHER ON SUNDAY?

We worship on Sunday because it is the most convenient day for us to get together and worship. In most areas of the world, Sunday has been set aside for this purpose. Sunday is considered the first day of the week and celebrated by the early church in memory of Christ' resurrection. *"Now on the first day of the week, when the disciples came together to break bread, Paul, ready to depart the next day, spoke to them and continued his message until midnight."* Acts 20:7 (NKJV)

"On the first day of the week let each one of you lay something aside, storing up as he may prosper, that there be no collections when I come." 1 Corinthians 16:2 (NKJV)

WHEN DO WE SIN AGAINST THE FOURTH COMMANDMENT?

We break the fourth commandment, because of unbelief. When, we fail to enter into rest that is found in the Lord Jesus Christ by faith. *"Therefore, while the promise of entering His rest still holds and is offered [today], let us be afraid to distrust it], lest any of you should think he has come too late and has come short of [reaching] it."* Hebrews 4:1 (AMP)

"Let us therefore be diligent to enter that rest, lest anyone fall according to the same example of disobedience." Hebrews 4:11

"Let us therefore be zealous and exert ourselves and strive diligently to enter that rest [of God, to know and experience it for ourselves], that no one may fall or perish by the same kind of unbelief and disobedience [into which those in the wilderness fell]." Hebrews 4:11 (AMP)

SUNDAY SCHOOL QUESTIONS

Q1. WHY DO WE WORSHIP TOGETHER ON SUNDAY?
Q2. WHEN DO WE SIN AGAINST THE FOURTH COMMANDMENT?

> **Memory Verse:**
> *"Let us therefore be diligent to enter that rest, lest anyone fall according to the same example of disobedience."* Hebrews 4:11

Prayer:

1. Lord Jesus! Take away the spirit of restlessness from me!

2. Every door of my prosperity that has been shut, be opened now.

3. Lord, convert my poverty to prosperity, in the name of Jesus.

4. You stones of hindrance, planted at the edge of my breakthroughs, be rolled away now, in Jesus' name. *5.*

You stones of stagnancy, stationed at the border of my life, be rolled away now, in the name of Jesus. *6.*

My God, let every stone of the wicked planted at the beginning of my life, at the middle of my life and at the end of my life; be rolled away now, in the name of Jesus. *7. Father*

Lord, I thank You for all the stones You have rolled away. I forbid their return, in the name of Jesus. *8. O Lord My*

God! Let Your power from above come upon me.

9. Forgive me O Lord of my unbelief in the name of Jesus. Amen!

9. Lord God Almighty! Help my unbelief in the name of Jesus!

10. O God give me the grace to have great faith in Jesus' name!

11. I come against the spirit of doubt and unbelief in Jesus' name. Amen!

12. Begin to thank God.

LORD! MAKE ME SPEND MY YEARS IN PLEASURE!

A man comes to me with tales of woes about his financial situation. His story was that of hardship and struggles he had been and still involved in many of his endeavors. But tried as much as he could; he said; it had been impossible to make ends meet. His financial situation was simply a complete mess even though he was born again. After hearing him out, I took time to educate him on the basic principles of tithing and sowing seed of faith. But try as I may, I could not convince him. For every scripture I cited, he had a reason why he cannot apply God's principle. He claimed if 100% can't pay the bills how then 90% can? He said the principles I am telling him are not likely to help because he has been hearing them for a very long time coming.

After the session with him, I understood why he had not and may never breakthrough financially by godly means. From his reaction to the counsel, it was obvious that he was not obedient to God's counsel for prosperity. That is the way many Believers are. Whereas, they want all the good things that God promised, they prefer not to fulfill the conditions attached to such promises. If you are one of them, it is time for you to change. God's capacity to bless is limitless. What is limited is man's capacity to receive the blessings of God. Obedience to the word of God is what increases your receptive capacity. What is it you desire? Is it wealth, divine health, influence and affluence? You can open God's treasure box by obeying Him, as you abide by His dictates, you shall spend you days in prosperity and pleasure.

Prayer: *I receive now the grace to obey the counsel of God!*

I SHALL RECEIVE MERCY!

I believe that Blind Bartimaeus must have been a spiritually sensitive man. Else, how did he know exactly what to say to draw the attention of Jesus? Bartimaeus could have been shouting and screaming "Jesus of Nazareth open thou my eyes." He could have cried Jesus of Nazareth, heal me now please." He could even have said a lot of other things that would have had no impact. But he cried thus; Jesus of Nazareth have mercy on me." Even when the people tried to shut him up, he shouted even more the same words with vehemence. Surely, he must have known that mercy covers all sins. He must have been aware that mercy understands, mercy sympathizes and leads to forgiveness. Mercy prevails over justice and judgment. He must have thought that mercy was the only thing that could touch a chord in the heart of Jesus to make Him break protocol for his sake. And according to his faith and desire, he received his sight.

Saint! What is it you desire? Is it healing, breakthrough, favor, blessings, deliverance etc., whatever it is, you can access it if you receive the mercy of God. Is your life a sad story of struggles and sufferings? Ask right now for God's mercy. And I pray that by the reason of these anointed words of God that you are reading now, the mercy of God is coming upon you in Jesus' name. And as you ask for God's mercy you shall receive guaranteed answers to your heart desires in Jesus' name!

Prayer: *Lord Jesus! Have mercy upon me this day and grant my heart's desires in Jesus' name. Amen!*

October 15th

The Word Today: Mark 11:1-8

I PROPHESY! MY TIED DOWN BLESSINGS ARE NOW RELEASED!

The story of the young donkey in our text-passage is a symbol of Jesus Christ deliverance power over the power of darkness and bondage. Luke 4:18. A donkey is designed and destined to carry people and stuffs from place to place. But the colt could not fulfill its destiny because it was tied down. Obviously, it could not move beyond the circumference and length of the rope tying it to the stake or pole. Many people's life is like that of the donkey. The enemy has tied them down with invisible spiritual ropes and cords so that they cannot exceed certain level of achievement in their lives. The passage states that the colt was not only tied down in a public place but that certain individuals were watching over it to make sure that it was not untied, to make sure the status of the donkey never change for good. That is the strategy of the enemy. The intention is that the colt remains a public disgrace.

Maybe the enemy has plagued you with harassing and embarrassing afflictions that have made you a laughing stock. Maybe you have not been able to exceed a certain level of achievement in your life. Maybe like the colt, certain powers or making-sure-demons are monitoring you to ensure you are never free from the vicious circle of your issues. I come to declare to you this day the counsel of God! You are delivered in the name of Jesus. And everything tying you down is loosed now in Jesus' name. Amen!

Prayer: *I decree every evil chain in my life is broken in the name of Jesus. Amen!*

133

October 16th

The Word Today: 1 Samuel 16:11-13

"... And the LORD said, Arise, anoint him: for this is he. Then Samuel took the horn of oil, and anointed him in the midst of his brethren..."

I PROPHESY! I SHALL BE DIVINELY RECOMMENDED!

If Jesse was to recommend one of his sons for the throne, it would definitely not have been David. But David became king because he was divinely recommended by heaven. I prophesy you shall receive divine recommendation for supernatural elevation. The good Lord will choose to use you in Jesus' name!

Secularly, when you have recommendations from highly placed individuals to apply for positions, you have an edge over others. And in most cases, you succeed, because the interviewers give regards and credence to your referees. However, even though there is a good chance of success for those who get recommended from great people, human recommendations do sometimes fail. But there is no room for failure when you have heaven's backing. With divine recommendation, there is no negative report. That is what happened in the case of David. Even though all his brothers were there before him, none could succeed because heaven had approved David for the position. Saint, I tell you this, this season you will step into uncommon favor in the name of Jesus. It does not matter whether you have someone in high position or not. You will be called upon to execute that contract you applied for, that business opportunities will come your way, and you shall be lifted up above others in Jesus' name. Amen!

Prayer: *Oh Lord God of David, like you did for David, recommend me for promotion in Jesus' name. Amen!*

GOD'S JUDGMENT AGAINST ME IS AVERTED!

When Josiah learnt that the Lord had passed judgment on Israel because of the sins and iniquities of their fathers; he went into deep prayers and supplications interceding on their behalf. And God postponed the judgment of death and destruction which he had passed on the children of Israel until after King Josiah's death. God stayed the judgment and averted the calamity of the people. Amen!

So also many people have the judgment of God awaiting them even before they are born. This is because the sins and iniquities of their forefathers have laid wrong and faulty foundations for them to build on. These faulty foundations cause evil occurrences and misfortunes in their lives. And until these faulty foundations are destroyed and rebuilt, such people would always have calamity in their endeavors. Calamity becomes their identity. But this shall no longer be your portion in the name of Jesus. Amen!

Are you one of such people? Have you been marked for destruction because of sins of your fore parents? This day like King Josiah, I intercede on your behalf in prayers and supplication onto God for His mercy upon you in Jesus' name. Amen! The mercy of the LORD God shall come on you and any negative judgment against you is hereby averted in Jesus' gracious name. Amen!

Prayer: *O Lord My God! I plead for Your mercy! Deliver me from every negative judgment in Jesus' name. Amen!*

135

WORD SWORD OF THE ORACLE

The Word Today: Exodus 27:1

"You shall make an altar of acacia wood, five cubits long and five cubits wide—the altar shall be square—and its height shall be three cubits."

ALTAR [HEBREW] *MIZBEAH*

Altar *[Mizbeah]* in the Hebrew language as used in Exodus 27:1, Exodus 30:1 Strong's concordance #4196. This word depicts a "place of slaughtering" and is derived from the verbal root meaning "to slaughter for sacrifice" Exodus 20:24, Deuteronomy 16:2. The Greek rendition is thusiasterion pronounced *[qusiasthvrion]*.

Altars are site of sacrificial worships Genesis 8:20, and were made of earth Genesis 20:24, stones Joshua 8:31, Judges 13:19 or even of bronze Exodus 38:1-7. An altar is a structure on which offerings are made to a deity. In the developed temple ritual, the same word is used for both the altar of holocausts and the altar of incense. Thus, an altar is a place where sacrifice is offered, even if it is not an event involving slaughter. The ritual slaughtering of animals to God was central to Hebrew worship at the temple Leviticus 1:5. But throughout Scripture, the God warned that righteousness, justice and a humble heart submitted to God are more important than bringing sacrificial gifts to the altar Psalm 51:17, Proverbs 21:3, Matthew 5:23-24. The sacrifices on the altar in the temple were a sign that God had forgiven the Children of Israel their sins. That sign pointed to the ultimate sacrifice: the sacrifice of His Son on the Cross for our sins. Hebrews 9:11-15, Hebrews 13:10-13.

3rd Sunday of the Month of October

CHURCH AND HOME SUNDAY SCHOOL

THE SECOND TABLE OF THE LAW

THE FIFTH COMMANDMENT

WHAT IS THE FIFTH COMMANDMENT?

"Honor your father and your mother, that your days may be long upon the land which the Lord your God is giving you." Exodus 20:12 (NKJV)

WHY DOES GOD ADD THE PROMISE
"THAT IT MAY BE WELL WITH THEE AND THOU MAYEST LIVE LONG UPON THE EARTH"?

By this promise, God impresses upon us the importance and benefit of honoring our parents and superiors and urge us to obey this commandment willingly. *"Children, obey your parents in the Lord [as His representatives], for this is just and right. Honor (esteem and value as precious) your father and your mother—this is the first commandment with a promise. That all may be well with you and that you may live long on the earth."* Ephesians 6:1-3 (AMP)

WHAT DOES GOD REQUIRE OF US IN THE FIFTH COMMANDMENT?

God requires us to: 1] Honor our parents and elders through obedience, love and respect. And also our spiritual leaders who are God' representatives on earth: *"Children, obey your parents in the Lord [as His representatives], for this is just and right. Honor (esteem and value as precious) your father and your mother—this is the first commandment with a promise. That all may be well with you and that you may live long on the earth."* Ephesians 6:1-3 (AMP)

137

Leviticus 19:32 (NKJV) *"You shall rise before the gray headed and honor the presence of an old man, and fear your God: I am the Lord."*

BIBLE NARRATIVES:

1. JOSEPH HONORED HIS FATHER JACOB IN Genesis 46:29
2. KING SOLOMON HONORED HIS MOTHER IN 1 Kings 2:19
3. ELISHA HONORED HIS TEACHER/MENTOR ELIJAH IN 2 Kings 2:12

God also requires us to: 2] Serve our parents by gladly doing what we can for them and helping them when they are in need. *"But if any widow has children or grandchildren, let them first learn to show piety at home and to repay their parents; for this is good and acceptable before God."* 1 Timothy 5:4 (NKJV)

BIBLE NARRATIVES:

a. JOSEPH PROVIDED FOR HIS FATHER: Genesis 47:11-12
b. JESUS PROVIDED FOR HIS MOTHER: John 19:26-27

God requires us to: 3] Obey our parents in all things that are not sinful. *"Children, obey your parents in the Lord [as His representatives], for this is just and right.* Ephesians 6:1 (AMP)

"Listen to your father who begot you, and do not despise your mother when she is old." Proverbs 23:22 (NKJV)

BIBLE NARRATIVES:

a) JESUS WAS SUBJECT TO MARY AND JOSEPH: Luke 2:41-42

b) JONATHAN DISOBEYED HIS FATHER IN ORDER TO SPARE DAVID'S LIFE AND THUS OBEYED GOD RATHER THAN MAN: 1 Samuel 20:31-33.

God requires us to: 4] Respect and obey all lawful superiors. All authority comes from God. When God places people in authority over us, He expects us to obey them. If we refuse to obey lawful superiors such as parents, teachers, pastors, government officials etc; we refuse to obey God. *"Therefore submit yourselves to every ordinance of man for the Lord's sake, whether to the king as supreme, or to governors, as to those who are sent by him for the punishment of evildoers and for the praise of those who do good."* 1 Peter 2:13-14

"[You who are] household servants, be submissive to your masters with all [proper] respect, not only to those who are kind and considerate and reasonable, but also to those who are surly (overbearing, unjust, and crooked)." 1 Peter 2:18 (AMP)

SUNDAY SCHOOL QUESTIONS

Q1. WHAT IS THE FIFTH COMMANDMENT?
Q2. WHY DOES GOD ADD THE PROMISE "THAT IT MAY BE WELL WITH THEE AND THOU MAYEST LIVE LONG UPON THE EARTH"? Q3. WHAT DOES GOD REQUIRE OF US IN THE FIFTH COMMANDMENT?

Memory Verse: "Honor your father and your mother, that your days may be long upon the land which the Lord your God is giving you." Exodus 20:12 (NKJV)

Prayer:

Lord! Help me obey my biological and spiritual parents in all things in the name of Jesus. Amen!

139

The liberal soul shall be made fat; and he that watereth shall be watered also himself."

I SHALL ACCUMULATE WEALTH AS I DESTRIBUTE TO OTHERS!

*T*he above text-verse above teaches us a great lesson; that to get, is to give; to accumulate, is to scatter; to make ourselves happy, is to make others happy; and that in order to become spiritually and physically energetic, you must seek the spiritual and physical well being of others. How is this so? For your efforts to become useful and bring out your usefulness, your latent talents and dormant faculties must be exercised to bring them to light. Your strength is hidden even from yourselves, until you venture to fight the Lord's battles, and climb the mountains of difficulty.

You do not know what tender sympathies you possess until you dry the widow's tears, and soothe the orphan's grief. You gain, when you instruct others through their pain. You learn great lessons at others' sick beds! And watering others humbles you. Your comfort is increased by your working for others comfort. When you endeavor to cheer people up, the consolation gladdens your own heart. Like the poor widow of Zarephath in 1 Kings 17:8-16, she gave from her scanty store to supply the prophet's needs, and from that day she never again knew lack. Luke 6:38 says Give and it shall be given unto you, good measure, pressed down, shaking together and running over shall men give unto your bosom. Give bountifully now and receive abundantly in Jesus' name. Amen!

Prayer: *Lord! Give me the grace to give bountifully!*

The Word Today: 2 Samuel 12:26-30

I PROPHESY! I SHALL WALK INTO GREATNESS!

Indeed, David was a man who had everything going for him. He was so blessed and favored that people denied themselves blessings and honor in order to render such accolade to him. The event in our text-passage above was one of such examples. While David enjoyed the comforts of his palace, Joab risked his life in a battle against Rabbah. Just when victory was assured, Joab paused. And instead of conquering the city and taking it over for himself, he sent a messenger to King David and said, in verse 27 and 28 of 2 Samuel 12 *"I have fought against Rabbah, and I have taken the city's water supply. Now therefore, gather the rest of the people together and encamp against the city and take it, lest I take the city and it be called after my name."*

Accordingly, David moved in and took over the city and brought forth the spoils of the city in great abundance in verse 30. Do you desire such? Saint I prophesy to you this day that you shall step into greatness and great accruing abundance in the name of Jesus. Amen! By the anointing of the Spirit of God upon me, I decree and smear on you the oil of favor. As you accept, believe and receive this by faith, the angels of God whose task, it is to fulfill the counsels of the messenger of the Lord will move on your behalf. This is your season to walk into ready-made miracles in the name of Jesus. Amen! Be expectant for you will be jubilant in this season of jubilee in the name of Jesus. Amen!

Prayer: *Oh God of David, I call upon You now; direct and lead me into my breakthrough in Jesus' mighty name. Amen!*

October 22nd

The Word Today: 1 Kings 17:8-16

I AM RELEASED INTO MY SEASON OF DIVINE PROVISION!

*W*henever God wants to bless His people, He sends His word by His prophets to declare breakthrough on them. On your part, you are expected to activate the covenant of prosperity established in Genesis 8:22. Those who understand and apply this principle always reap bountifully from heaven's warehouse of blessings. Saul understood this principle that is why he asked his servant what they would give to Prophet Samuel when they meet him. 1 Samuel 9:7. Solomon also knew and used this key to activate the greatest prosperity known to man 2 Chronicles 1. It was that same key that Elijah used to activate in the life of the widow of Zarephath, divine provision by asking her to sow into his life. As the Oracle of God, I have the divine mandate to lead people into their divine provision. This day, I charge you to avail yourself of the following opportunity. One of the media which God has given me to carry out the mission of liberation in this generation is this publication: [THE ORACLE OF GOD DEVOTIONAL]. For this cause, anyone who partner with me to expand this work globally surely becomes a beneficiary of covenant increase which I enjoy. Today, I challenge you to activate your own season of divine provision by prayerfully considering entering into partnership with me. You can do so by committing yourself to buying and distributing this book to at least 5 people or donate any amount towards the publication. If you do so faithfully, I decree this day that the anointing for remarkable results is coming upon your life now in Jesus' name! 2 Chronicles 20:20.

Act now,

October 23rd

The Word Today: Isaiah 8:9-10

"Associate yourselves, O ye people, and ye shall be broken in pieces; and give ear, all ye of far countries: gird yourselves, and ye shall be broken in pieces; gird yourselves, and ye shall be broken in pieces. Take counsel together, and it shall come to nought; speak the word, and it shall not stand: for God is with us."

EVERY DEMONIC ASSOCIATION AGAINST ME IS BROKEN!

1 Thessalonians 5:19-21 says *do not quench the Spirit. Do not despise prophecies. Test all things; hold fast what is good.—*

This is a crude illustration, but let me tell you what we did after planting a field of corn when I was a young in the village in Africa. To save the field of corn from the crows, we would shoot an old crow and hang it by its heels in the middle of the field. This was supposed to scare off all of the crows for miles around. The crows would hold a conference and say, "Look, there is a field of corn but don't go near it. There is a dead crow over there!" That's the kind of conference that Satan calls, and that is exactly what he has done. He has taken some Believers who do things that they shouldn't, and he has stationed them in the middle of God's cornfield, and warns, "Now, don't you go near that doctrine about the Holy Spirit because if you do, you will act just like those "I pray the Lord keep us, from shying away from such valuable truth and experience as the ministry of the Holy Spirit because of the excesses of a few wrong ones. May we not lose too much, and we can't afford the loss in Jesus' name. Amen."

Prayer: *O Lord! Deliver us from demonic manipulations!*

143

The Word Today: 2 Chronicles 32:19-20, (NLT) Isaiah 37:4.

"These officers talked about the God of Jerusalem as though he were one of the pagan gods, made by human hands. Then King Hezekiah and the prophet Isaiah son of Amos cried out in prayer to God in heaven."

GOD WILL RESPOND TO MY REQUEST WITH DIVINE SPEED!

The speed of God's response to the supplication of His children is a function of certain factors which include; the spiritual stature of the supplicant/petitioner, the intensity or earnestness of the prayer and the power of agreement with a prophet of the most High.

In the scripture above, these factors worked in unity to produce immediate result. Hezekiah was a man of great spiritual stature. He needed an urgent answer to his request. So, the request was made with utmost earnestness. But perhaps, the most effective factor that influenced an instant answer to his request was that Prophet Isaiah, a major prophet and an Oracle of God, who was of very great spiritual stature, stood in the gap and in agreement with the king. Today, I stand as a major prophet of God to prophesy in agreement with you, the Lord shall answer your prayers speedily in Jesus' name. Amen! I want you to ask God three major things you want Him to do for you this season in all earnestness. And as you do, I join my faith with yours in agreement; I call on heaven to release your answer speedily in Jesus' name. The God of Isaiah and Hezekiah shall honor my words by releasing your answer this time in Jesus' name!

Prayer: *I join my faith with the faith of the Prophet to decree; a release of answers to my request in Jesus' name. Amen!*

WORD SWORD OF THE ORACLE

The Word Today: Exodus 30:18 (NKJV)

"You shall also make a laver of bronze, with its base also of bronze, for washing. You shall put it between the tabernacle of meeting and the altar. And you shall put water in it."

WASHING [HEBREW] *RACHATS*

In Exodus 2:5, Exodus 30:18, Proverbs 30:12 as in Strong's concordance #7364 is the Hebrew word *Rachats* which, means washing or bathing. This term has very important cultural and religious value associated with it. The ancient custom of washing a guest's feet was an act of hospitality that lasted into the New Testament period Genesis 18:4, John 13:5.

Ritual washing was an important step in the purification of the priests for service in the tabernacle Exodus 40:12. Washing with water symbolized spiritual cleansing, the preparation necessary for entering God's presence Psalm 26:6, Psalm 73:13. The Old Testament prophets continued to use this imagery of washing and applied it symbolically to act of repentance Isaiah 1:16, Ezekiel 16:4. In the New Testament, Paul the Apostle describes redemption in Christ as "the washing of regeneration" Titus 3:5.

The act of washing for consecration or for purification from uncleanness involved washing all or part of the body or one's clothing. Jesus Christ's attitude to the Pharisees reflected, not a disapproval of ritual washing, but disapproval of their emphasis on the outward, rather than inward forms of religion.

Prayer: *Lord Jesus! Wash me in and out with the washing of Your word and Your Blood in the name of Jesus. Amen!*

4ᵗʰ Sunday of the Month of October

CHURCH AND HOME SUNDAY SCHOOL

WHEN ARE WE NOT REQUIRED TO OBEY PARENTS OR SUPERIORS?

When someone in authority attempts to use that authority to have us do something sinful or forbids us to follow God.

"But Peter and the other apostles answered and said: "We ought to obey God rather than men." Acts 5:29 (NKJV)

WHAT ARE THE DUTIES OF PARENTS TOWARD THEIR CHILDREN?

Parents are required to care physically and especially spiritually to meet the needs of their children, this is very important. They should teach them to pray, praise and worship God and read His word always. Parents must work to inculcate and develop in their children the values of obedience, truthfulness, respect, cleanliness, etc. They are also required to care for the physical, mental and emotional needs of their children. Parents are not to provoke their children to wrath.

"And you, fathers, do not provoke your children to wrath, but bring them up in the training and admonition of the Lord." Ephesians 6:4 (NKJV)

"Do not withhold correction from a child, for if you beat him with a rod, he will not die. You shall beat him with a rod, and deliver his soul from hell." Proverbs 23:13-14 (NKJV)

WHAT ARE OUR DUTIES TO OUR COUNTRY?

We must love our country, we must be sincerely interested in its welfare and respect and obey its laws and pray for our country and its leadership.

146

WHY MUST WE OBEY THE LAWS OF OUR COUNTRY?

The lawful authority of our nations comes from God, the source of all authority, and we must be obedient to Him [God]. If certain laws are contrary to God's word, we are duty bound to disobey them.

BIBLE NARRATATIVES:

1. THE THREE HEBREWS [SHEDRACK, MESHACH AND ABEDNIGO IN DANIEL 3
2. DANIEL IN THE LION'S DEN IN DANIEL 6.

WHAT DOES GOD FORBID IN THE FIFTH COMMANDMENT?

God forbids disobedience, disrespect and unkindness towards parents and superiors. Be it spiritual or secular.

"The eye that mocks his father, and scorns obedience to his mother, the ravens of the valley will pick it out, and the young eagles will eat it." Proverbs 30:17 (NKJV)

BIBLE NARRATIVES:

1. THE SONS OF ELI GRIEVED THEIR FATHER BY THEIR WICKEDNESS: 1 SAMUEL 2:12-15
2. ABSALOM REBELLED AGAINST HIS FATHER KING DAVID: 2 SAMUEL 15.

SUNDAY SCHOOL QUESTIONS

Q1. WHEN ARE WE NOT REQUIRED TO OBEY PARENTS OR SUPERIORS?
Q2. WHAT ARE THE DUTIES OF PARENTS TOWARD THEIR CHILDREN?
Q3. WHAT ARE OUR DUTIES TO OUR COUNTRY?
Q4. WHY MUST WE OBEY THE LAWS OF OUR

COUNTRY? Q5. WHAT DOES GOD FORBID IN THE FIFTH COMMANDMENT?

> ## Today's Memory Verse
> "The eye that mocks his father, and scorns obedience to his mother, the ravens of the valley will pick it out, and the young eagles will eat it." Proverbs 30:17 (NKJV)

Today's Prayer:

1. *O Lord My Father! Give me the grace to obey my parents in the name of Jesus. Amen!*

2. *Forgive me O Lord! In any way I have been disobedient to my biological and spiritual parents and elder!*

3. *Father! Release the blessing of long life and prosperity upon me in the name of Jesus. Amen!*

4. *You carry-over miracle from my past fasting and prayer program, receive the touch of fire and materialize.*

5. *Holy Ghost fire, baptize me with prayer miracle.*

6. *Every area of my life that needs deliverance, receive the touch of fire and be delivered, in the name of Jesus.*

7. *Let my angels of blessing locate me now, in Jesus' name.*

8. *Every satanic program of impossibility, I cancel you now.*

9. *Every household wickedness and its program of impossibility be paralysed, in the name of Jesus.*

10. *No curse will land on my head, in the name of Jesus.*

11. *Throughout the days of my life, I will not waste money on my health; God shall be my healer, in Jesus' name.*

THE WORK OF MY HANDS SHALL YIELD GREAT INCREASE!

The spiritual truths embedded in our word today are so deep that it deserves further attention. The reason many people work so hard without result is either because they are not receiving proper spiritual meal or they are not living in complete obedience to God's word. In the scripture above, God promise us shepherd for divine directions to guide and instruct us on what to do to receive God's blessings and provisions.

So when you do not follow your God ordain shepherd, you are in danger of being cut off from God's divine blessings and provisions. Also if you refuse to follow the directives of your shepherd, you will lose out on your divine benefits. Are you in such situation now? If so, I release the grace of God upon you now, be restored in the name of Jesus. Amen! God has rules and patterns; and He also has blessings for everyone. All you have to do is to locate and obey your shepherd to receive yours. As you do so, and comply with God's directives, consequently the works of your hands shall be blessed with divine increase. I do not know what you are going through right now, maybe, you have experienced failure and hardship all your life. Today I stand as a divine shepherd over God's people and with the delegated authority from the good Shepherd Jesus Christ; I prophesy the curse of hardship in your life is broken!

Prayer: *O God! Let the works of my hands yield great increase in the mighty name of Jesus Christ!*

The Word Today: Psalm 50:14-15

"Offer unto God thanksgiving; and pay thy vows unto the most High: And call upon me in the day of trouble: I will deliver thee......"

GOD WILL ANSWER ME SPEEDILY AS I FULFILL MY VOWS!

The most important thing about vow in Psalm 50:14-15 is, if you call on God in the day of trouble He will surely answer and deliver you and you shall glorify Him. But in verse 14 you will see the condition on which the verse operates and depends. Psalm 50:14 says "Offer unto God thanksgiving and pay thy vows unto the most high and call upon me in the day of trouble, and I will deliver thee and thou shalt glorify me." Now if you don't speed read the bible, if you read the scriptures carefully, you will observe that, at the end of verse 14 there is no full stop. The point here is that, the story continues onto verse 15. It said you must do two things. First, offer unto God, thanksgiving: Secondly pay your vows unto the most high and then call on the Lord in the day of trouble. He will surely deliver you and you will glorify Him.

I want you right now to make a vow. I have made several vows before and I can tell you one thing, God has never failed on His word. I want you to bow your heads for a few minutes and challenge the Almighty! Say, *"Father do this for me and I will do that for you."* Talk to Him for a while; just tell Him, Father, I know that You are the Almighty, there is nothing You cannot do. You are a covenant keeping God, You are a faithful God answer me speedily this day.

Prayer: *Lord! Answer and deliver me speedily in Jesus' name!*

"For when for the time ye ought to be teachers, ye have need that one teach you again which be the first principles of the oracles of God; and are become such as have need of milk and not of strong meat."

I PROPHESY! MY SPIRITUAL GROWTH IN JESUS' NAME!

For all Believers who desire meaningful spiritual growth in their walk with God; there is no height you cannot attain in the spirit if only you are ready to take the bull by the horn. If you will put away every form of ungodliness and follow the principles of spiritual growth laid down in God's word. Hebrews 5:12 says *"For when for the time ye ought to be teachers, ye have need that one teach you again which be the first principles of the oracles of God; and are become such as have need of milk and not of strong meat."*

Our Lord and savior Jesus Christ expects us to grow to the level where we can teach others. In many of the Epistles, we are encouraged to grow in grace and in the knowledge of Christ 2 Peter 3:18. When a Believer refuses to grow, he remains a spiritual babe who is unskillful in the word of God. Such baby Christians needs milk and not strong meat. When we begin to apply these truths in our lives, we will begin to grow and our knowledge of Christ will also increase. Paul encourages the Believer to be "rooted and built up in Him" Colossians 2:7. As Believers, we draw our nutrients from Jesus Christ. As you pray the prayer below for spiritual growth, the Holy Spirit will draw you into a deeper and fulfilling relationship with Christ Jesus.

Prayer: *O God, help me comprehend the breadth, length, depth and height of the love of Christ, in the name of Jesus.*

The Word Today: Isaiah 45:19

"....I said not unto the seed of Jacob, Seek ye me in vain."

I PROPHESY! I WILL NOT SEEK THE LORD GOD IN VAIN!

𝔗he promises of God are full of comfort and delight; what he has not said is scarcely less rich in consolation. You may gain much solace by considering what God has not said. It was one of these "said nots" which preserved the kingdom of Israel in the days of Jeroboam the son of Joash, for *"the Lord **said not** that he would blot out the name of Israel from under heaven."* 2 Kings 14:27.

In our text-verse above you have an assurance that God will answer prayer, because He hath *"not said unto the seed of Israel, Seek ye me in vain."* Even if you say evil things against yourself, what you say will not cut you off from God's mercy. There is no room for despair: even the voice of conscience is of little weight, if it be not seconded by the voice of God. What God has said, tremble at! But suffer not your vain imaginings to overwhelm you with despondency and sinful despair. Many timid persons have been vexed by the suspicion that there may be something in God's decree which shuts them out from hope. God has clearly revealed that He will hear the prayer of those who call upon him, and that declaration cannot be contravened. He does not reveal His mind in unintelligible words, but he speaks plainly and positively, *"Ask and ye shall receive."* Believe, and your prayers shall be answered in Jesus' name. Amen!

Prayer: *Lord Jesus! I will not seek You in vain so bless me indeed in Jesus' name. Amen!*

The Word Today: 1 John 1:8-9

"If we say that we have no sin, we deceive ourselves, and the truth is not in us. ⁹ If we confess our sins, He is faithful and just to forgive us our sins and to cleanse us from all unrighteousness."

GOD WILL HEAL ME AS I CONFESS AND REPENT OF MY SINS!

There is an old tale of a king who visited a prison. He spoke with the prisoners, and each man claimed to be innocent, a victim of the system. Only one man, however, sat silently in a corner. And then the King approached him and asked him, "And you, sir, who do you blame for your sentence?" The prisoner said, "Your majesty, I am guilty and deserve my imprisonment."

Surprised, the king called for the chief warden: "Come and get this man out of here before he corrupts all these innocent people." The King of Kings can set you free once you admit your fault. You do yourselves no favors in justifying your sins.

Believers are like a five year old kid that got a splinter in his finger. When the parent applies iodine, and a Band-Aid, he didn't like what he saw and said Mummy "I just want the Band-Aid to cover the wound but no iodine." We come to Christ with our sin, but all we want is a covering.

We want to skip the treatment. We want to hide our sin. But God, even in his great mercy, will not heal what we conceal. Proverbs 28:13 says *"Whoever conceals their sins does not prosper, but the one who confesses and renounces them, finds mercy."* How can God heal what we deny? How can God touch what we cover up? How can we have communion with Him while we keep secrets? How can God grant us pardon when we won't admit our guilt?

Are you one of such people who play the blame game? Blaming others but yourself for everything that is gone wrong with you? This is the time to change. Accept your guilt and be released from the bondage of sin and guilt. Guilt isn't what we avoid? Guilt, isn't what we detest? But guilt does implies that we now know right from wrong, that we aspire to be better than we were, that we know there is a higher life and we are in the lower level now but desire to go higher and become better. That's what guilt is: it is a healthy regret of telling God one thing and change to doing another which is right in His sight.

Guilt is the nerve ending of the heart. It yanks us back when we are too near the fire. Godly sorrow "makes people change their hearts and lives. This leads to salvation, and you cannot be sorry for that" 2 Corinthians 7:10. To feel guilt is no tragedy; to feel no guilt is. If you have not yet surrendered your life to Jesus, you cannot invite God to release you from your prison of guilt. You cannot ask for divine intervention until you confess and admit your faults, repent of such sins and ask God for forgiveness. And restitute when possible. There is power in the blood of Jesus to set you free and cleanse you from all unrighteousness. If you want and decide to give your life to Christ now, please say the following prayer."

PRAY THIS BELIEVERS' PRAYER NOW!

Father, in the name of Jesus, I come before you now. I acknowledge that I am a sinner. Forgive my sin and cleanse me with your blood. I renounce and denounce the devil and all his works. Come into my life Lord Jesus and take absolute control of my life, BE MY Lord and Savior in Jesus' name I pray. Amen!

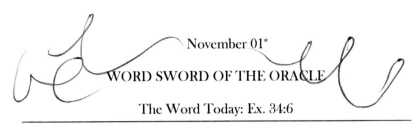

"And the Lord passed by before him, and proclaimed, The Lord, the Lord God, merciful and gracious, longsuffering, and abundant in goodness and truth."

GOODNESS [HEBREW] *CHESED*

The Hebrew word *Chesed* means Goodness as used in Exodus 34:6, Exodus 20:6, Strong's #2617. When God revealed Himself to Moses on Mount Sinai, He described Himself as overflowing *goodness* [*Chesed*] in the Hebrew. This is one of the most significant words that describe God's character Psalm 13:5. It is often translated as *Mercy* Exodus 20:6, Psalm 6:4 and sometimes as *Lovingkindness* Psalm 17:7.

The basic meaning of the word *Chesed* is "Loyal Love" or "Steadfast Love." It connotes God's loyalty and faithfulness to His covenant. This love is very similar to marital love, a love that is obligatory because of marriage contract, but still intimate and voluntary. Hosea's action toward his unfaithful wife is a striking picture of God's "faithful and unfailing love" for the people of Israel. Hosea 1:1-3, Hosea 2:19, Hosea 3:1-5. In the New Testament this characteristic of God is described as His grace [Greek *Charis* John 1:17] The English root word for charisma.

Here some Bible verse on good and goodness: Psalm 31:19, Romans 8:28, Psalm 23:6, Psalm 145:15-19, Galatians 5:22-23, Rom. 12:9, James 3:13, Gal. 5:22, John 3:16-17 Micah 6:8, James 1:17, Ps. 27:13, Ps. 25:7, Gal. 6:10, Ps. 65:4, 2 Tim. 3:16, Matt. 12:35, Ps. 34:8, Titus 3:8-10, Matt. 5:28-29, 2 Peter 1:5, 1 Tim. 1:5, 1 Thess. 5:21, Jer. 29:11, Rom. 3:10-12, Acts 7:51, Ex. 33:19.

CHURCH AND HOME SUNDAY SCHOOL

THE SIXTH COMMANDMENTS

WHAT IS THE SIXTH COMMANDMENTS?

"You shall not murder." Exodus 20:13 (NKJV)

WHAT ARE WE COMMANDED BY THE SIXTH COMMANDMENTS?

We are commanded to properly care for the spiritual and physical welfare of ourselves and neighbors and to show them love by respecting their person and not injuring them in any way or form.

WHAT DOES GOD FORBID IN THE SIXTH COMMANDMENT?

1. God forbids us to kill or to injure our neighbor by murder, fighting etc; to take life by abortion, our own life by suicide or neglect of our health.

"But Jesus said to him, "Put your sword in its place, for all who take the sword will perish by the sword." Matthew 26:52 (NKJV)

Note that the government has the right to inflict the death penalty and to wage just war.

2. God forbids us to do or say anything which may destroy, shorten or embitter our neighbor's life. *"Beloved, do not avenge yourselves, but rather give place to wrath; for it is written, "Vengeance is Mine, I will repay," says the Lord."* Romans 12:19

3. God forbids anger, hatred, revenge, recklessness and bad example. *"But I say to you that everyone who continues to be angry with his brother or harbors malice (enmity of heart) against him shall be liable*

to and unable to escape the punishment imposed by the court; and
Whoever speaks contemptuously and insultingly to his brother shall
be liable to and unable to escape the punishment imposed by the
Sanhedrin, and whoever says, You cursed fool! [You empty-headed
idiot!] Shall be liable to and unable to escape the hell (Gehenna) of
fire. "Matthew 5:22

"Anyone who hates (abominates, detests) his brother [in Christ] is
[at heart] a murderer, and you know that no murderer has eternal life
abiding (persevering) within him. " 1 John 3:15 (AMP)

"For out of the heart come evil thoughts (reasoning and disputing
and designs) such as murder, adultery, sexual vice, theft, false
witnessing, slander, and irreverent speech. "Matthew 15:19 (AMP)

"Be angry, and do not sin" do not let the sun go down on your
wrath. "Ephesians 4:26 (NKJV)

WHAT DOES GOD REQUIRE OF US IN THE SIXTH COMMANDMENT?

1. We should be merciful, kind, forgiving towards our neighbors.
"Blessed are the merciful, for they shall obtain mercy. Blessed are the
pure in heart, for they shall see God. Blessed are the peacemakers,
for they shall be called sons of God. "Matthew 5:7-9 (NKJV)

"But if you do not forgive men their trespasses, neither will your
Father forgive your trespasses. "Matthew 6:15 (NKJV)

"And be kind to one another, tenderhearted, forgiving one another,
even as God in Christ forgave you. "Ephesians 4:32

2. We should help and befriend our neighbors whenever we can.

"But a certain Samaritan, as he journeyed, came where he was. And
when he saw him, he had compassion. So he went to him and
bandaged his wounds, pouring on oil and wine; and he set him on his

own animal, brought him to an inn, and took care of him. On the next day, when he departed, he took out two denarii, gave them to the inn keeper, and said to him, 'Take care of him; and whatever more you spend, when I come again, I will repay you.' Luke 10:33-35 (NKJV)

BIBLE NARRATIVES:

1. ABRAHAM RESCUED LOT: GENESIS 14:12-16
2. DAVID PROTECTS THE LIFE OF KING SAUL: 1 SAMUEL 26:1-12

SUNDAY SCHOOL QUESTIONS

Q1. WHAT IS THE SIXTH COMMANDMENT?
Q2. WHAT ARE WE COMMANDED BY THE SIXTH COMMANDMENT?
Q3. WHAT DOES GOD FORBID IN THE SIXTH COMMANDMENT? Q3. WHAT DOES GOD REQUIRE OF US IN THE SIXTH COMMANDMENT?

> **Memory Verse:** "You shall not murder."
> Exodus 20:13 (NKJV)

Prayer:

Lord! Forgive all my trespasses of your commandment in Jesus' name. Amen!

MY DESTINED GREATNESS SHALL MANIFEST AS I PRAISE GOD!

*Y*our destiny is about to change today as you praise God in Jesus' name! David said, in Psalm 34:1-3 when he pretended to be insane before Abimelech who drove him out. He said *"I will bless the Lord at all times; His praise shall continually be in my mouth."* God responded and said, "In that case David, your kingdoms shall be established forever." I prophesy, to you this day as your praise ascends unto God, your greatness shall never descend in the gracious name of Jesus. Amen!

PRAISE JEHOVAH EL-SHADDAI NOW:
Glorify be to You Holy Name Lord! I Praise You from the bottom of your heart! You are the Alpha and the Omega; the beginning and the ending, the One who was, the One who is, and the One who will ever be! The Almighty God! The Unchangeable Lord! My Redeemer! My great Physician! My miracle-working God! Your name is Wonderful! Counselor! Mighty God! The Prince of Peace, The Everlasting Father, The Rock of Ages; the Lion of Judah! I adore You! Blessed be Your Holy Name in Jesus' name!

NOVEMBER BIRTHDAY AND WEDDING ANNIVERSARY PRAYERS

Father I commit all Your children born in November and those celebrating their wedding day this month into Your hand. Lord, I ask that as they begin a new year in their lives, everything that is old, replace it with something new in Jesus' name. Give them new beginning of joy, new beginning of blessings, new breakthroughs.

The Word Today: 2 kings 3:5-20

"For thus says the Lord: 'You shall not see wind, nor shall you see rain; yet that valley shall be filled with water, so that you, your cattle, and your animals may drink.' Verse 17

I DECREE! I SHALL RECEIVE DIVINE PROVISION THIS DAY!

King Jehoram of Israel and his allies set out to war against Moab without consulting God. As a result, they lost their way in the desert. After days without water, it dawned on them that they were about to lose the military campaign to thirst. Then, King Jehoshaphat of Judah remembered the LORD and suggested they should seek divine direction from the Oracle of God, Prophet Elisha. And as they did, Elisha prophesied that out of nowhere God will provide water for them and He did. The Lord will provide for you also this day in the name of Jesus. Amen!

Saint! The lack you are experiencing right now, may be as a result of you not seeking the face of the LORD before embarking on whatsoever you are struggling with now. It may be your business, career, marriage etc. If you will make a U-turn and ask God for direction, He would change things for you for good. Just like the three kings did not know how and where the water came from I prophesy, you will receive divine provision from divine sources in the name of Jesus. Amen! All you have to do is to dig the ditch; which is, to prepare yourself for the miracle by believing this prophecy and be expectant. Then the LORD God will surprise you this season in Jesus' name. Amen!

Prayer: *Jehovah Jireh! The great provider! Provide for me this day in the name of Jesus. Amen!*

The Word Today: Job 14:7-9

I PROPHESY! THERE IS HOPE FOR ME!

You may have been written off by those around you. You may even consider your case hopeless and helpless. The doctors' report may have dimmed your hope. Some prophets may have prophesied doom for you. You may have gotten to your wits end and the word of hope and encouragement no longer ignites faith in you anymore. But I come to declare to you this day that, there is hope for you if you can read this message. And that is what the LORD God is saying to you in the word today. There is no hopeless case with God, but people who have lost hope. The worst thing that can happen to you is to lose hope. When you get to that condition of hopelessness, you lack the will to survive or succeed and as a result you tend to accept failure as your portion. Invariably, that which is accepted begins to manifest in your life. That is why the Bible says "as a man thinketh in his heart, so is he....." You fail as you think failure!

Have you lost all hope? Are you at the verge of giving up on life? Hear ye the counsel of the God of Job this day! All you need is the anointing of the Holy Spirit of God to change your circumstances for good, and anything that is dead or seemingly dead in your life is coming back to life now in the name of Jesus. Therefore, I release that anointing on your spirit man now to revive hope in you for a turnaround breakthrough in the name of Jesus. Amen! As you accept and believe this prophecy in faith, according to your faith, so shall it be in Jesus' name. Amen!

Prayer: *I charge my spirit man to come out of the doldrums of hopelessness in Jesus' name Amen!*

"...And he said, thou hast asked a hard thing: nevertheless, if thou see me when I am taken from thee, it shall be so unto thee; but if not it shall not be so."

I SHALL BE READY WHEN MY BREAKTHROUGH COMES!

$\mathscr{I}$ read and re-read the story of Elijah and Elisha without fully understanding the enormity of Elijah's charge to Elisha until the Spirit of the LORD enlightened me. Many would argue that what Elijah told Elisha, his protégé to do was not a difficult task, but a critical analysis of the charge proves otherwise. Agreeing to fulfill Elijah's condition meant a lot of responsibility for Elisha. The implication is that, he had to be vigilant and keep Elijah within his view 24/7. It meant he could neither sleep nor rest wholesomely until the translation of Elijah. It meant that as long as Elijah remained with him, Elisha could not focus on any other thing but his master. What a task?

Is that not a difficult condition? Surely it is. Many people are unable to secure their miracles because of lack of concentration. They pray and fast for breakthrough, they wait patiently for it to happen. But sometimes in a momentary lack of focus and concentration, they lose the manifestation of their testimonies to distractions. Such people need to pray for alertness of mind and of the spirit to encounter divine intervention. Are you one of such people? If so, I hereby release heavenly alertness upon you now. And I prophesy... you shall be ready when your miracle comes in Jesus' mighty name. Amen!

Prayer: *I tap into the grace to wait till the end, as was upon Elisha. Henceforth, I shall be ready for my miracle in Jesus' name.*

November 07th

The Word Today: Matthew 21:18-21

*"...And seeing a fig tree by the road, He came to it a
nothing on it but leaves, and said to it, "Let no fruit grow on you ever
again." Immediately the fig tree withered away......."*

EVERY ROOT OF UNFRUITFULNESS IN MY LIFE IS WITHERED!

On His way from Jerusalem to Bethany Jesus became hungry. He saw a fig tree from a distance and was expectant. But His expectation was dashed when He discovered that there was no fruit on the tree. In anger, He cursed the tree and it withered. The reaction of Jesus Christ to this; is very instructive as to God's intolerance for unfruitfulness. God expects us to bear fruits of success, prosperity, multiplication, and productivity etc.

Like Jesus was angry with the tree, so also God gets infuriated each time He sees unfruitfulness in our lives; because such unfruitfulness negates His original plan for man in Genesis 1:26-28. With His pronouncement on the tree, Jesus laid down a pattern to us about how to remove unfruitfulness from our lives. Is there any area of your life that is not producing good results? Now is the time to reverse that trend. Like Jesus did, you have the power in your tongue to curse out every curse in your life. Now lay your right hand on your head and begin to curse out, the unfruitfulness in your endeavors in the name of Jesus. Call them by name and curse them out of your life; poverty, barrenness, failure, near success syndrome, curses and spells etc. Begin to reverse them now in the name of Jesus. And as you do so, every root of unfruitfulness in your life is withered away!

Prayer: *Every root of unfruitfulness in my life is withered now in the
name of Jesus. Amen!*

WORD SWORD OF THE ORACLE

The Word Today: Exodus 25:9 (NKJV)

"According to all that I show you, that is, the pattern of the tabernacle and the pattern of all its furnishings, just so you shall make it."

TABERNACLE [HEBREW] *MISHKAN*

𝒯ℎe Hebrew word *Mishkan* as used in Exodus 25:9, Exodus 26:1, Exodus 40:2 Strong's concordance #4908; signifies "a dwelling place" and it is related to the verb meaning "to dwell", "to settle down" and "to live among" a temporary place to live, a tent. Songs Of Solomon 1:8. The Tabernacle was the portable dwelling place for God's presence from the time of the Exodus of the Israelite from Egypt and through the conquering of the land of Canaan. It was built to the specifications revealed by God to Moses at Mount Sinai. It accompanied the Israelites on their wanderings in the wilderness and their conquest of the Promised Land. The Tabernacle has an inner shrine- the Holy of Holies, housing the Ark of the Covenant and an outer chamber – the Holy Place, with a golden lamp-stand, a table for the showbread, and altar of incense; it is a simple tent-sanctuary.

God's tent, the tabernacle, functioned as an object lesson in God's holiness and a symbol of His divine presence among His people Exodus 33:7-11. It was a sign that God wanted to live among His people and establish an intimate relationship with them Exodus 5:8-9. The ultimate out-working of that desire was Jesus Christ, who was Himself God, became a man. As the son of God, Jesus lived among us, walked with us, and revealed God the Father to us John 1:14-18. This is why His name is Immanuel meaning God with us Matthew 1:23.

2ⁿᵈ Sunday of the Month of November

CHURCH AND HOME SUNDAY SCHOOL

THE SEVENTH COMMANDMENT

WHAT IS THE SEVENTH COMMANDMENT?

"You shall not commit adultery." Exodus 20:14 (NKJV)

WHAT IS THE MEANING OF ADULTERY?

Adultery is having sexual relations with someone other than the marriage partner.

Note here the expansion of the meaning of the seventh commandment includes whoredom in all its forms, as well as un-chastity [premarital relations, sexual impurity, and lustful desire under whatever name.] (J.P. Lange).

Not only is adultery forbidden here, but also fornication and all kinds of mental and sensual uncleanness. All impure books, songs, pictures, shows, movie etc., which tend to inflame and debauch the mind are against this law (Adam Clarke).

WHAT IS MARRIAGE?

Marriage is the lifelong union of one man and one woman.

Because marriage was instituted by God, married couples are required to love and honor each other unselfishly, to be faithful to each other, to provide for the welfare of their children and surrender themselves to the service of God. By following God's plan for marriage, the love between husband and wife should become a regular reflection of the love of Jesus Christ for His bride; the Church.

"Therefore, just as the church is subject to Christ, so let the wives be to their own husbands in everything. Husbands, love your wives, just as Christ also loved the church and gave Himself for her." Ephesians 5:24-25 (NKJV)

"So then, they are no longer two but one flesh. Therefore what God has joined together, let not man separate." Matthew 19:6

BIBLE NARRATIVES:

1.   THE INSTITUTION OF MARRIAGE: GENESIS 2:18-24

WHY IS ADULTERY A SIN?

Adultery is breaking of God's Law, as well as the violation of the marriage vow [commitment]. Marriage is the foundation of society and with it the responsibility of child rearing. Casual sex outside of marriage not only imperils marriage, it also disrupts and destroys the paternal or maternal feelings for the children of the marriage. The lines of inheritance and family relationships may become so confusing until children feel they have no identity.

WHAT IS FORNICATION?

The word fornication has two definitions: [the specific and general definition].

1.   Sexual intercourse between two unmarried people.
2.   The word fornication is a translation of the Greek word "PORNEIA" which is the root word for pornography, fornication includes all sexual acts outside of marriage such as: adultery, fornication, homosexuality, incest and bestiality.

SUNDAY SCHOOL QUESTIONS

Q1. WHAT IS THE SEVENTH COMMANDMENT?
Q2. WHAT IS THE MEANING OF ADULTERY?
Q3. WHAT IS MARRIAGE?
Q4. WHY IS ADULTERY A SIN?
Q5. WHAT IS FORNICATION?

Today's Memory Verse

"You shall not commit adultery." Exodus 20:14 (NKJV)

Today's Prayers:

1. *T*hank God for his power to deliver from every bondage sexual sin.
2. I break myself free from every spirit of sexual perversion.
3. I release myself from every spiritual pollution emanating from my past sins of fornication and sexual immorality.
4. I release myself from every ancestral sexual pollution.
5. I release myself from every sexual dream pollution.
6. I command every evil plantation of sexual perversion in me to come out with all its roots in the name of Jesus. Amen.
7. Every spirit of sexual perversion working against me, be paralyzed and get out of my life in the name of Jesus. Amen.
8. Every demon of sexual perversion assigned to my life, be bound, in the name of Jesus. Amen!
9. O Lord, let the power of sexual perversion oppressing my life receive the fire of God and be roasted, in Jesus' name.
10. Every inherited demon of sexual perversion in me, receive the arrows of fire and remain permanently bound.
11. I command every power of sexual perversion to come against itself, in the name of Jesus. Amen!
12. Begin to thank God for the blood of Jesus!
13. Thank God for the work Christ finished on the cross!

November 10th

The Word Today: Job 42:10-11

I PROPHESY! THIS IS MY SEASON OF RECOMPENSE!

As you pray today the Lord will turn your captivity around for good in Jesus' name. Amen! Before God allowed the devil to afflict Job, Job was a man of great wealth. So great was his substance of wealth that it exert a pull of envy of everyone in the land even Satan. And the affliction caused him to lose all that he had- health, wealth, children, power, everything was gone. The misfortune is enough for anyone to lose faith in God but not Job, Job held on to God. Not even his wife and friends' caricaturing could make him stop trusting God. He kept waiting for a better day and the day came as God rewarded Him double for all his trouble.

Have you lost all that you had? Are you a shadow of what you use to be or ought to be? Have you become a subject of ridicule in your vicinity because of your afflictions? I admonish you to keep the faith, keep trusting the Lord for better days are on the way for you. Change is coming for you. Have hope, for hope is essential in the miracle making process. Until you lose hope, Satan cannot triumph over you. Had Job lost hope, His story would have been entirely different. But as he kept on hoping and trusting in God, the LORD moved on his behalf. The good God of Job will also move on your behalf as you faithfully hope and trust in Him. He will turn your captivity around for good. Just have a rekindled hope in God for this is your season of reparation in Jesus' name!

Prayer: *O God of Job, turn around my captivity this day!*

168

The Word Today: 2 Kings 4:38-44

"Then they served it to the men to eat. Now it happened, as they were eating the stew, that they cried out and said, "Man of God, there is death in the pot!" And they could not eat it. So he said, "Then bring some flour." And he put it into the pot, and said, "Serve it to the people, that they may eat." And there was nothing harmful in the pot."

EVERY EVIL DEPOSIT IN MY BODY IS DESTROYED!

The sons of the prophet had unknowingly consumed some poisonous herb. Then they cried out unto Elisha, the Oracle of God saying *"O man of God there is death in the pot"* verse 40. And so it was that Elisha neutralized the power of the poison in the pot with the power of the anointing of God upon him.

You may have been poisoned physically and or spiritually in the dream. Maybe the enemy has deposited poison in your body through satanic incisions and injections in the dream. Or you may have been struck with some astral projectiles, evil arrows and bullet in the dream. That has caused terrible health issue for you or/and your loved ones. But that must end today!

Whatever it may be, I stand as the Oracle of God and declare that any evil implantation in your body, spirit and soul is hereby neutralized and destroyed in the mighty name of Jesus! Just like the poison in that pot became harmless after Elisha added meal, every harmful substance the enemy has deposited in your system is hereby rendered harmless by the anointing of the Holy Spirit in the name of Jesus. Amen!

Prayer: *Every demonic deposit in me is destroyed in the name of Jesus. Amen*

The Word Today: Psalm 37:1-5

GOD WILL GRANT ME MY HEART'S DESIRES!

In Psalm 37:1-5 David was not just saying words he had heard or read somewhere, but he was talking about things he had experienced in life. At a point in his life, when King Saul chased him all over the land, it seemed as though the *'Good had lost to Evil'*. At various times when Saul had David surrounded, it appeared that the counsel of God for his life would not be fulfilled. Even when his family and belongings were sacked and carted away by hoodlum at Ziklag, it appeared the desire of his heart would never come to pass. But David always trusted God. He committed all his action and thought into the hands of God.

In the end God proved Himself, faithful and mighty in the life of David by making him overcome all his enemies and all the adverse conditions of his life. I pray for you that, like David, you too will overcome your adverse situation in the name of Jesus. Amen! But you have to trust and hope absolutely on God. Trust and obey God for there is no other way to be happy in Jesus. And this is the test many believers fail in their quest to get their heart's desire in life. When you lose hope and resign yourself to fate then you lose your miracle. If, you begin to seek help from ungodly sources, disappointment will set in. Are you one of such people? Saint, have you been visiting unholy and ungodly places to seek what they call practical solution to your problems? You have to retrace your steps now; God is working out your miracle. If you believe and just hope and trust in Him you will have your heart's desire in Jesus' name. Amen!

Prayer: *Lord! Grant me grace and faith to wait for my miracle!*

November 13th

The Word Today: Psalm 121:1-8

"I will lift up my eyes to the hills from whence comes my help? My help comes from the Lord, who made heaven and earth."

I KNOW MY HELP WILL COME FROM GOD!

When faced with problems many run around looking for help where there is none at all! Quite often, people who ordinarily should know better, turn to satanic practices like soothsaying, psychics, juju, voodoo, hoodoo, witchcraft and wizardry because of pressures of life. In most cases, they end up worse than they were before they sought for such help. They are ignorant of the devices of the devil and his agents. And they never realize that the enemy does not offer any good or free gift. Beloveth, I do not know what mistakes you may have made while seeking help from strange and ungodly places in the past. Maybe you have tread where you should not or done what you should not do. And entered into evil covenants thereof; but today, I stand in the office of the Oracle of God to declare that help is coming from the Lord for you in the name of Jesus Christ!

So, I enjoin you now to repent and come back to Jesus, for He is the only One that can give you the help you desire, "for vain is the help of man..... Psalm 108:12. It is better to put your confidence in God rather than man. Man will always fail or/and want something in return for whatever help they render, but the gift of God is overwhelming love and grace. As you look up to heaven, the Lord of Host will guide you, and will not allow you to fumble nor stumble in Jesus' mighty name. Amen!

Prayer: *O God forgive my waywardness; guide my path and send me help from above in Jesus' name. Amen!*

171

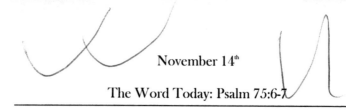

November 14th

The Word Today: Psalm 75:6-7

"For exaltation comes neither from the east. Nor from the west nor from the south. But God is the Judge: He puts down one, and exalts another."

DIVINE PROMOTION IS COMING MY WAY THIS TIME!

Do you believe and agree with the above prophecy? If so, then declare the following severally before you continue with the devotion: *"I accept the divine promotion that is coming my way in the name of Jesus." "I key into the anointing for supernatural lifting and I am moving higher and forward to the next level in Jesus' mighty name." Amen!* As you accept, believe and receive this prophecy, the positive forces of heaven that are responsible for arranging promotion for those favored by God would go to work to ensure that you are lifted far above where you are right now! The promotion you desire is neither in the hands of your boss, your manager or supervisor but with God. So, instead of seeking their approval, seek God's favor, the boss of all bosses.

All that David needed was to be on the side of God to be lifted. Accordingly, God divinely arranged a position at the top for him in the palace. I like you to know that when God favors you, there is no need to seek after positions. Instead positions will begin to seek you out. I don't know what you are thinking right now. Perhaps, you have lost hope and may have even accepted the position you find yourself presently. Saint, I want you to know that it is never over until God says it is. So, I prophesy divine promotion is your portion in Jesus' mighty name. Amen!

Prayer: *Father Lord! Release the anointing for divine favor upon me and my loved ones in Jesus' name. Amen!*

November 15th

WORD SWORD OF THE ORACLE

The Word Today: Leviticus 1:2 (NKJV)

"Speak to the children of Israel, and say to them: 'When any one of you brings an **offering** *to the Lord, you shall bring your* **offering** *of the livestock—of the herd and of the flock."*

OFFERING [HEBREW] *GARBAN*

As used in Leviticus 1:2, Ezekiel 20:28 Strong's #7133. The Hebrew word *Garban* meaning offering, is derived from the verb "to bring near" and it literally means "that which one brings near to God." The fact that the Israelite had such an opportunity to present their gifts to God reveals His mercy. Even though they were sinful and rebellious, God instituted a sacrificial system in which they could reconcile themselves to Him. Jesus' death on the Cross of Calvary was the ultimate offering that ended the need for all that in this dispensation. For through the sacrifice of His sinless life, we have once and for all been reconciled to God.... Hebrews 10:10-18. An appropriate response to Jesus' death for us is to offer our lives as living sacrifice unto God... Romans 12:1.

Here are some scriptures about Tithes and Offering: Prov. 11:24-26, Mark 12:41-44, Luke 6:38, 2 Cor. 9:6-7, Prov. 3:9-10, Ps. 4:5, Matt. 6:1-4, Acts 20:35, 1 Cor. 16:2, Luke 16:10, Luke 21:1-4, Philipp. 4:19, 2 Cor. 8:1-15, Matt. 6:33, Matt. 6:21, Rom. 13:7, Luke 11:42, Deut. 14:22-29, Gen. 28:20-22, 1 Cor. 9:13-14, Mal. 3:1-18, Ps. 50:7-12, Luke 18:12, Deut. 16:17, 2 Chr. 31:5-12, 1 Cor. 13:3, Ex. 25:2, 1 Tim. 5:17-18, Haggai 2:8, Ps. 24:1, Acts 11:27-29, Amos 4:4-5, Acts 4:34-35, Eccl. 5:4-5, John 3:16, Deut. 18:4, Gal. 6:9, 2 Cor. 1:1-24, Deut. 8:17-18, 1 Cor. 16:1-2, Deut. 26:12-13, Matt. 5:23, Isa. 40:9, Num. 18:20-31, Genesis 14:1-24, Nehemiah 12:44, 1 Corinthians 9:14, 2 Timothy 3:16-17.

3rd Sunday of the Month of November

CHURCH AND HOME SUNDAY SCHOOL

WHAT IS WRONG WITH PRE-MARITAL SEX?

Sex outside of marriage is a sin against your own body and against God; because your body is the temple of the Holy Spirit. The Bible commands us to flee fornication as a sin against ourselves and against God.

"What? Know ye not that your body is the temple of the Holy Ghost which is in you, which ye have of God, and ye are not your own?" 1 Corinthians 6:19-20

So if the Believer takes his body and joins it to a harlot [someone immoral] he is actually joining Jesus Christ to that immoral person. The Bible clearly teaches that neither fornicators nor adulterers will enter into the kingdom of heaven.

"Now the works of the flesh are evident, which are: adultery, fornication, uncleanness, lewdness, idolatry, sorcery, hatred, contentions, jealousies, outbursts of wrath, selfish ambitions, dissensions, heresies, envy, murders, drunkenness, revelries, and the like; of which I tell you beforehand, just as I also told you in time past, that those who practice such things will not inherit the kingdom of God." Galatians 5:19-21 (NKJV)

Today, the term fornication is rarely used, and immorality between unmarried people across all age group; young and old is a widely accepted and expected lifestyle. But immorality, however commonplace it is, is still a sin. Unless repentance is sought and forgiveness is received, it will keep millions of people out of God's Kingdom. Galatians 5:19-21.

WHAT IS HOMOSEXUALITY AND WHY IS IT A SIN?

*H*omosexuality is any sexual activity between men with men or women with women. Men who burn with lust for other men are called Homosexuals [Gays]. Women who burn with lust for other women are called Lesbians [Gays]. *"You shall not lie with a male as with a woman. It is an abomination."*Leviticus 18:22

The Bible calls homosexuality an abomination [too vile to talk about]. In the Old Testament, this sin was punishable by death. And these days you see all manner of sexual perversions in gay men and women being ordained ministers of God, which is great sacrilege. Repentance must be sought or destruction cometh. *"If a man lies with a male as he lies with a woman, both of them have committed an abomination. They shall surely be put to death. Their blood shall be upon them."* Leviticus 20:13

In the New Testament we are told that those who practice homosexuality and lesbianism will not enter the Kingdom of God. From a Biblical standpoint, the rise of homosexuality and all forms of sexual perversions is a sign that a society is in the last stage of decadence. *"For this reason God gave them up to vile passions. For even their women exchanged the natural use for what is against nature. Likewise also the men, leaving the natural use of the woman, burned in their lust for one another, men with men committing what is shameful, and receiving in themselves the penalty of their error which was due."*Romans 1:24-27 (NKJV)

"Do you not know that the unrighteous will not inherit the kingdom of God? Do not be deceived. Neither fornicators, nor idolaters, nor adulterers, nor homosexuals, nor sodomites, nor thieves, nor covetous, nor drunkards, nor revilers, nor extortioners will inherit the kingdom of God." 1 Cor. 6:9-10

WHAT IS INCEST AND WHY IS IT A SIN?

Incest is a sexual perversion and a sinful act between closely related persons: parents with their children, brothers with sisters, and relatives with family members. It is a moral sin. Leviticus 18:6-14

Some parents actually feel justified in using their children for sexual gratification, just because they belong to them. God hates this wickedness with a passion. These parents either lack parental love or are ignorant of the deep emotional scares they inflict upon their children. Many of these innocent victims are tormented with guilt and feelings of worthlessness, making them emotionally incapable of coping with life. *"Love does no harm to a neighbor; therefore love is the fulfillment of the law."* Romans 13:10

SUNDAY SCHOOL QUESTIONS

Q1. WHAT IS WRONG WITH PRE-MARITAL SEX?
Q2. WHAT IS HOMOSEXUALITY AND WHY IS IT A SIN?
Q3. WHAT IS INCEST AND WHY IS IT A SIN?

> **Memory Verse:** "You shall not lie with a male as with a woman. It is an abomination." Leviticus 18:22 (NKJV)

Prayers:

1. *Father Lord, let every demonic stronghold of sexual sin in my life be pulled down in the name of Jesus.*

2. *Every power of sexual perversion that has consumed me shattered to pieces in the name of Jesus.*

3. *Lord delivered me from the forces of sexual perversion.*

November 17th

The Word Today: Psalm 30:11 and Ecclesiastes 3:1-4

MY MOURNING IS TURNING TO DANCING THIS DAY!

The Lord God knows all you are going through; for He is Omniscient; when you do not have a dime in your pocket, He knows; when you went to bed hungry and angry, He knows. He is aware of all the bitterly cold winter you've being through without heat. God knows that your kids' fees are in arrears unpaid. He knows and sees all. He knows and wants you to also know that there are times for mourning. He knows that there is a time when things will not work out as you planned or expected, when things seem to go wrong in spite of proper planning. He knows all this because He is Omniscient.

Nevertheless, there is also a time for dancing. So, the Lord of all seasons and times, has asked me to declare to you that today, your days of mourning is turning to days of dancing in the name of Jesus. Amen! As the seasons of the earth exist, so also is your own season of dancing and celebrating starts. You may be wondering how this can be. I am sure because God cannot lie. I am confident because out of the mouth of two or three witnesses, the word is established. The Spirit of God has declared it through the Psalmist, David and King Solomon that after mourning; comes laughter. So, I declare to you this day, your mourning is becoming dancing in the name of Jesus! Today, the word of God that is forever settled in heaven will be forever established in your life in the name of Jesus. Amen!

Prayer: *My days of mourning are over in Jesus' name. Amen!*

177

EVERY BROKEN AREA OF MY LIFE IS RESTORED!

Elijah was one man that understood spiritual principles very much. That is why he recorded outstanding results in his walk with God. In our text-verse above, he exhibited his insight into the workings of the Almighty God when he began by repairing the altar of God. Before then, influenced by King Ahab and his wife Queen Jezebel, the Israelites had neglected God for a long time. They had destroyed the altars of God, and replace them with those of Baal. So to rekindle God's interest in them, Elijah knew that they had to appease Him. So, he engaged the people in the rebuilding of the altar. That is why God answered him expressly by fire. Amen!

Many people are unable to attract God's attention because there are some areas of their lives that are broken down and in disrepair. For some it is their prayer life, for others their fasting life, yet for some they have neglected the word of God, some lack in their faith in God. Are you one of such people? I declare to you this day, every area of your life that is in disrepair shall be repaired in the name of Jesus. Amen! Saint! The God we serve is the same God of Elijah. He is not a respecter of persons but that of principles. It is almost impossible to attract God's attention with such anomalies as broken prayer alters, sinful lifestyles, lack of fellowship etc. Do you desire to attract God's attention like Elijah did? Take a look at your life, put aside sinful habits, reconcile yourself unto God and it shall be well with you!

Prayer: *Lord! Repair every area of my life that is in disrepair in Jesus' name. Amen!*

November 19th

The Word Today: Job 42:10-12 (NKJV)

"And the Lord restored Job's losses when he prayed for his friends. Indeed the Lord gave Job twice as much as he had before. Now the Lord blessed the latter days of Job more than his beginning; for he had fourteen thousand sheep, six thousand...."

THE LORD GOD SHALL TURNAROUND MY CAPTIVITY!

The story of Job is a testimony of fact; that God is Omnipotent. Sometimes, He allows you to go through difficulties to glorify His name in your life. For years on end Job suffered torment and degradation in the hands of the devil. He lost his wealth, his health, all his children and every good thing in life that he had, he was harassed and embarrassed; yet he still trusted in God. And when God decided it was time to show up and show out for Job, He *"....turned the captivity of Job" around and "blessed the latter end of Job more than his beginning."* Job 42:12.

Is your story as sad as Job's story? Have you lost everything you once had? Have your family and friends forsaken you because of series of failures? Have you started querying your faith in God because of your struggles and sufferings? Saint! Hear the Word of God, henceforth the Lord God will turn your captivity around like He did for Job in the name of Jesus! Whatsoever you may have being going through, is just a phase in your life, it started one day, and it must certainly end one day and that day is today in the name of Jesus. Amen! I pray that henceforth you begin to rejoice as you experience your victory over the power of darkness in the name of Jesus. Amen!

Prayer: *Lord! Let goodness and mercy follow me all the days of my life in Jesus' name. Amen!*

179

GOD WILL GIVE ME INSIGHT TO HIS SECRET PLANS!

What make a person influential in life are insights. You are likely to remain unsung in your endeavor until you begin to get information that others don't have. For instance, in organizations, the person(s) that wields the most powers are not usually those whose rankings follow that of the boss but those who have the confidence of the boss. This is because such people always know of the plan(s) of the boss before others. Such vantage positions always put them ahead of others. The Almighty God is the boss of the universe, so when you become favored by Him, you automatically become a powerful and a person of relevance. That is what happened to Elijah.

In our text-verse above, it is obvious that with or without Elijah, God would have still release rain upon the earth. In fact, the tone of the message means that God had already done so. However, in order to make Elijah relevant, He gave him an insight into His plan. In the same vain God told Abraham of His plan to destroy Sodom and Gomorrah in Genesis 18:17-33. Thus Abraham and Elijah became great. I do not know what you do or what you aspire to become. But the key to your elevation lies in your stand with God. If He considers you right enough to reveal His plans, then your blessings would know no bounds. Do you desire greatness in life? If you do, then get closer to God. Deuteronomy 29:29 says that He is the custodian of all secrets. The secret of all that you desire is with God. If you humble yourself and ask, He will give you insight into His secret!

Prayer: *O God of Elijah! Give me insight to make me great!*

The Word Today: Isaiah 40:1-5

"Prepare the way of the Lord; Make straight in the desert a highway for our God. Every valley shall be exalted. And every mountain and hill brought low. The crooked places shall be made straight. And the rough places smooth; the glory of the Lord shall be revealed, and all flesh shall see it together; for the mouth of the Lord has spoken."

THE ROUGH AREAS OF MY LIFE SHALL BE SMOOTHENED!

Saint, I have good news for you this day. Every rough area in your life shall be smoothened. The mouth of the Lord has spoken it and it shall surely come to pass in Jesus' name. Amen! Rough places; stands for those areas in your life that are not going smoothly or functioning properly. For example, you may be wealthy, healthy and intelligent but unable to get married. That is a rough place. Some people may have children but may not be able to cater for them and that also is their own rough end. Yet some other people might have all these things but lack emotional and spiritual fulfillment. For such a person, his/her lack of emotional and spiritual fulfillment is their rough places.

Just like in our passage above, rough places may be a direct consequence of wrong doings (sins) and or curses. It is a source of sorrow to a person. But whenever Jesus steps into such situations, He pardons wrong doing(s), and makes rough places plain, and ultimately replaces sorrow with joy. That is your portion today in Jesus' name. Whatever it is that is your own rough place; I prophesy that rough place in your life is made plain now in Jesus' name. Amen!

Prayer: *I decree and declare that every rough edge in my life is straightened and made plain in Jesus' name. Amen!*

WORD SWORD OF THE ORACLE

The Word Today: Leviticus 2:2

"and take it to Aaron's sons the priests. The priest shall take a handful of the flour and oil, together with all the incense, and burn this as a **memorial portion** *on the altar, a food offering, an aroma pleasing to the Lord.*

MEMORIAL PORTION [HEBREW] *'AZKARAH*

The words Memorial Portion, *Azkarah* in Hebrew as in Leviticus 2:2, Leviticus 2:9, Leviticus 2:16 Strong's #234. Is a small portion of grain offering burnt on the altar in place of the whole sum; the rest was a gift to the priest, to support him in his ministry. The word for memorial portion is related to the Hebrew verb *Zakar*, which means "to remember." It signifies the worshipper's remembering of God's gracious character and generosity, especially God's remembering and blessing of the worshipper.

The Greek word for memorial as in Acts of the apostle chapter 10 is *mnēmosunon*, something that enables someone to remember. So if the memorial goes up before God, then it makes possible sense that it functions as a memorial for God to remember something about the one who gives the memorial.

But the Septuagint translates *'Azkarah'*, the *'memorial portion'* of the grain offering in our text-verse above "as the sign whereby the worshipper is reminded or taught that the whole offering is in fact owed to God but that He is pleased to accept only a part of it as a 'token' while remitting the burning of the rest of it on the altar so that it may be otherwise consumed."

Prayer: *Lord! Accept my 'memorial portion this day.*

4ᵗʰ Sunday of the Month of November

CHURCH AND HOME SUNDAY SCHOOL

WHAT IS BESTIALITY AND WHY IS IT A SIN?

*B*estiality is sexual relations between a person and an animal. It is an abominable sin of sexual perversion. It is a sexual perversion. *"Nor shall you mate with any animal, to defile yourself with it. Nor shall any woman stand before an animal to mate with it. It is perversion."* Leviticus 18:23 (NKJV)

WHAT DOES GOD FORBID IN THE SEVENTH COMMANDMENT?

1. God forbids the breaking of marriage vows by unfaithfulness or desertion. He permits the innocent party to procure a divorce when the other party is guilty of fornication and adultery and will not repent. *"Marriage is honorable among all, and the bed undefiled; but fornicators and adulterers God will judge."* Hebrews 13:4 (NKJV*)*

BIBLE NARRATIVES:

1) DAVID' ADULTERY WITH THE WIFE OF URIAH: 2 SAMUEL 11
2) HEROD TOOK HIS BROTHER'S WIFE: MARK 6:18

God forbids all sexual perversion and immorality. He cautions us to avoid immodesty, in words, in actions and looks, whether it is alone or with others. Examples of this would be sinful thoughts or desires, immodest dress or behavior, suggestive actions, filthy conversations, pornography, X-rated literatures, movies or plays to arouse desire for fornication and adultery.

"For out of the heart proceed evil thoughts, murders, adulteries, fornications, thefts, false witness, and blasphemies." Matthew 15:19

"But I say to you that whoever looks at a woman to lust for her has already committed adultery with her in his heart." Matthew 5:28.

"But fornication and all uncleanness or covetousness, let it not even be named among you, as is fitting for saints; neither filthiness, nor foolish talking, nor coarse jesting, which are not fitting, but rather giving of thanks." Ephesians 5:3-4 (NKJV)

"For it is shameful even to speak of those things which are done by them in secret." Ephesians 5:12 (NKJV)

BIBLE NARRATIVES:

1) POTIPHAR'S WIFE, LUST IN HER HEART, CAST HER EYES ON JOSEPH: GENESIS 39:7-12
2) SAMSON COMMITTED FORNICATION: JUDGES 16:1

WHAT DOES GOD REQUIRE OF EVERYONE IN THE SEVENTH COMMANDMENT?

God require us to lead a Christian life, beyond reproach and to be pure in our thoughts, desires, words and deeds. If we fall into any sexual sin, we need to repent by confessing and praying for forgiveness. Not only will God forgive us and cleanse us from our sins, but He will also deliver us from the evil lusts that caused us to yield to temptation. Deliverance from all sin and iniquity is available to earnest seekers.

"Finally, brethren, whatever things are true, whatever things are noble, whatever things are just, whatever things are pure, whatever things are lovely, whatever things are of good report, if there is any virtue and if there is anything praiseworthy—meditate on these things." Philippians 4:8 (NKJV)

"Let no corrupt word proceed out of your mouth, but what is good for necessary edification, that it may impart grace to the hearers." Ephesians 4:29 (NKJV)

SUNDAY SCHOOL QUESTION

Q1. WHAT IS BESTIALITY AND WHY IS IT A SIN?
Q2. WHAT DOES GOD FORBID IN THE SEVENTH COMMANDMENT?
Q3. WHAT DOES GOD REQUIRE OF EVERYONE IN THE SEVENTH COMMANDMENT?

> **Memory Verse:** *"Beloved, I beg you as sojourners and pilgrims abstain from fleshly lusts which war against the soul."* 1 Peter 2:11 (NKJV)

Today's Prayers

1. *F*ather Lord! Deliver me from the spirit of lust in Jesus' name!
2. Deliver me O God from sinful thoughts in the name of Jesus!
3. Holy Ghost fire, fall upon my eyes and burn to ashes every satanic power controlling my eyes in Jesus' name. Amen!
4. Lord! Deliver me from the spirit of fleshy lust in Jesus' name!
5. I move from sexual bondage to liberty in every area of my life in the name of Jesus.
6. I cover myself with the blood of Jesus, in Jesus' name!
7. Thank You Lord for answered prayers.

I DECREE AND DECLARE I AM MADE WHOLE!

" *What* you think you saw is not what you saw" It is common knowledge that everyone has one issue or the other bothering them at various points and periods in their lives. Many people's problems may not be obvious: there is more to them than meet the eyes. 'There is this adage that says all lizards lie prostrate, so one cannot judge which one has stomach ache'. So except a person tells you of his or her problem, you may not know about it. For some people, their problems are financial challenges, for others it may be health issues, for some, marital settlement or inability to procreate. In ministry, I have come across all kinds of issues of life. In fact, I have seen and heard so much to know that everyone needs to be made whole. I do not know what your area of need is, but I do know that there is someone who can do deeds to meet your every need. His name is Jesus! By the power that is in His name and His blood, I prophesy, you shall be made whole in the name of Jesus.

The woman with the issue of blood in Matthew 9:19-22 had the need to be made whole for a long time. For twelve whole years she bled excessively nonstop. And had become hopeless; she must have been waiting to die but then she heard Jesus was in town, hope and faith returned to her. She decided to receive her healing by touching the garment of Jesus and she got it immediately. I Prophesy, according to your faith so shall it be unto you in Jesus' name. Amen!

Prayer: *O God! Make me whole again in Jesus' name!*

MY PATH TO PROMINENCE SHALL BE REVEALED UNTO ME!

For every individual of destiny, there is always a defining moment when the path to glory is revealed. That moment is always marked with divine contact that opens your eyes to the glory ahead of you. For Saul, that contact was Prophet Samuel. Before that meeting, he had a low self esteem and inferiority complex. As a result, he was simply content with managing his father's flocks. But after spending some hours with the Oracle of God, his path to glory was revealed. From that day, he never looked back as he moved from one level to the next until he mounted the throne as the King of Israel. I declare, your path to greatness shall be revealed to you earnestly in Jesus' name!

However, before your path to prominence is revealed, there is always the tendency to spend energy on some distracting activities in the search of relevance. But the discovery of destiny's path comes with a rugged determination that leads to realization of desired goal. This is so, unto Saul's ascension to the throne. I pray that as the path of your glory is revealed to you, the same spirit that fell upon Saul would also fall upon you and move you faster to the glory that God prepared for you in Jesus' name. Amen! The realization of the path to your destiny comes with a strong conviction that renews commitment to the achievement of such goals. So, be alert for those ideas, hunches and thoughts that provoke you to move forward. As you do so, you will soon be on your path to greatness in Jesus' name!

Prayer: *O God! Reveal unto me, my path to greatness in Jesus' name. Amen!*

187

The Word Today: Psalm 40:1-3

I PROPHESY! I AM COMING OUT OF THE HORRIBLE PIT!

Have you been wallowing in the pit of life? Have you been stuck in the miry clay all your life? Have you been crying for mercy all your days? Saint! I have good news for you today; you are coming out of the horrible pit of life in Jesus' name. Amen!

A horrible pit signifies the low side of life, abject poverty, afflictions, infirmities, death etc. Perhaps the enemy has been showing you mental images of yourself in a pit, watery well, and finding yourself in coffins in your dreams. That is exactly how the enemy keeps people in the pit of life.

A man's circumstances are a product of images he has of himself. So, having known this, the enemy ensures that he projects negative images into the mind of the unguarded victims with which he keeps them bound. If you are a victim of such manipulations, I declare that this day you are coming out of that horrible pit in Jesus' name. Amen!

Maybe you are in the pit of financial crises, marital instability or spiritual and emotional emptiness. Maybe your own horrible pit is infirmities and afflictions. Whatever may be the case, I stand today as the Oracle of God, the servant of the King of kings and the Lord of lords to declare to you that your days of suffering and shame are over. Therefore, I decree you are coming out of that miry pit now in Jesus' mighty name. Amen!

Prayer: *Father Lord! By Your word I decree an end to a life in the horrible pit in the name of Jesus. Amen!*

I DECLARE! THE GLORY OF GOD IN MY LIFE SHALL BE REVEALED!

*I*magine the scenario in the passage above! A few verses earlier, Elijah was a fugitive, hiding from everybody. But in verse 40 of 1 Kings Chapter 18, he was giving the people instructions and strangely and surprisingly they obeyed him to the letter. That transformation took place simply because the glory of God in the life of Elijah was revealed. I decree this day that the glory of God shall be revealed in your life in the name of Jesus. Amen!

You know, normally, a person struggles for recognition until something happens to distinguish him or her from others. Until such happens, other people would naturally look down on you. That was the situation for Elijah. The people did not reckon with him until they saw the manifestation of the power of God in his life. I pray for you now, the glory and power of God shall be made manifest in your life this season in Jesus' name Amen!

All those who for many years have ridiculed you, very soon, they will see you celebrate your testimonies in Jesus name, they will see you in your marriage, with your children and in your own house, fully paid for in Jesus' name. Those who have written you off shall see you build your ministry and prosper in Jesus' mighty name. Amen!

Saint! It is time for people to see the might of God in your life. So prepare for divine elevation and promotion in the name of Jesus. God's glory shall be revealed in your life in the name of Jesus' name. Amen!

Prayer: *Lord! Make manifest Your glory in me in Jesus' name!*

189

November 28th

The Word Today: Acts 4:29

LORD, BEHOLD THE THREATENING OF MY ENEMIES!

In Acts 4, the apostles had been pushed around. They had been warned not to preach in the name of Jesus so they started praying: like this sister's testimony: *A sister said she had been born again for twenty-three years, but, right from the time that she started praying with us on the prayer conference; it was as if she had not been born again at all. She said despite the fact that the prayer points were strange, she prayed them any way, and she was getting results instantly for the first time in her Christian life and that, her life was never the same. According to her, since she joined this ministry, she no more seem to recognize what is called fear. When you say something big and terrible is happening, she just moved in and demolished it with prayer.*

This shall be you own testimony in the name of Jesus. Amen! She said several weeks back, somebody fired an arrow at her and one hand and one leg was getting paralyzed. And she applied the anointing oil, from the previous month three days marathon fasting on the affected area, and everything disappeared. And this sister is not a pastor nor is she a minister. She was only a member of the 'OGIM prayer conference. These are the kind of testimonies that encourage me. And not those who would say, "When my spouse was talking trash, I just gave him/her a dirty slap and later, asked God to forgive me." Pray thus:

Prayer: *My prayers shall bring good and great testimonies in the name of Jesus. Amen!*

190

WORD SWORD OF THE ORACLE

The Word Today: Leviticus 3:2 (NKJV)

*"And he shall lay his hand on the head of his offering, and kill it at the door of the tabernacle of meeting; and Aaron's sons, the priests, shall sprinkle the **blood** all around on the altar."*

BLOOD [HEBREW] *DAM*

The Hebrew word for blood is *Dam* as used in Leviticus 3:2, Leviticus 4:5, Exodus 12:13, Isaiah 1:11 Strong's #1818. The word *Dam* is closely related to the Hebrew word *Adom*, which means *'Red'* Genesis 25:30. And also refers to the blood of animals Exodus 23:18 or human beings Genesis 4:10. In the Scriptures, blood may be a synonym for death Judges 9:24 or even murder Jeremiah 19:4.

The word blood may also represent a person's guilt, as in the phrase "his blood shall be upon him"; that is, he is responsible for his own guilt Leviticus 20:9. The Old Testament equates life with blood Genesis 9:4, Leviticus 17:11, Deuteronomy 12:23, which vividly illustrate the sanctity of human life Genesis 9:6.

According to the New Testament "without shedding of blood there is no remission of sin" Hebrews 9:22. Thus the emphasis on blood in the Old Testament sacrifices, pointed to the blood of Jesus Christ that would be shed on our behalf on the Cross of Calvary. Romans 5:9, 1 Corinthians 11:25-26.

Blood is one of the most important studies in the Bible today. Starting from Adam to Cain and Abel, running through the Bible, making its application to us today very vital and even beyond to the glory of God!

5th Sunday of the Month of November

CHURCH AND HOME SUNDAY SCHOOL

WHY DOES GOD COMMAND US TO BE PURE AND MODEST IN ALL OUR ACTIONS?

God commands us to be pure and modest because as Christians our bodies are the temples of the Holy Ghost.

"Or do you not know that your body is the temple of the Holy Spirit who is in you, whom you have from God, and you are not your own? For you were bought at a price; therefore glorify God in your body and in your spirit, which are God's." 1 Corinthians 6:19-20

WHAT ARE THE PITFALLS WE SHOULD AVOID?

We are to avoid pitfalls, such as: idleness, bad companions, immodest dress, alcohol, narcotics, and X- rated entertainment: movies, television programming, books, and music. *"Create in me a clean heart, O God, and renew a steadfast spirit within me."* Psalm 51:10 (NKJV)

WHAT MUST WE DO TO LEAD A VICTORIOUS CHRISTIAN LIFE?

To lead a victorious Christian life, we must:

1) Fight to overcome all impure thoughts and desires by seeking God's help through prayer, fasting, studying and meditating on the word of God. *"Thy word have I hid in mine heart, that I might not sin against thee."* Psalm 119:11 (KJV)

2) By keeping busy in the Lord and by exercising self-control.

"There is no one greater in this house than I, nor has he kept back anything from me but you, because you are his wife. How then can I do this great wickedness, and sin against God?" Genesis 39:9 (NKJV)

"Do not look on the wine when it is red, when it sparkles in the cup, when it swirls around smoothly; at the last it bites like a serpent, and stings like a viper. Your eyes will see strange things, and your heart will utter perverse things." Proverbs 23:31-33.

3) We are to flee and avoid every temptation. Many fall because they do not avoid dangers. Human nature is very weak, especially where purity is concerned and we must avoid all occasions that can lead us into sin. *"Flee also youthful lusts; but pursue righteousness, faith, love, peace with those who call on the Lord out of a pure heart."* 2 Timothy 2:22 (NKJV)

"Flee sexual immorality. Every sin that a man does is outside the body, but he who commits sexual immorality sins against his own body." 1 Corinthians 6:18 (NKJV)

"My son, if sinners entice you, Do not consent." Proverbs 1:10

SUNDAY SCHOOL QUESTIONS

Q1. WHY DOES GOD COMMAND US TO BE PURE AND MODEST IN ALL OUR ACTIONS?
Q2. WHAT ARE THE PITFALLS WE SHOULD AVOID?

Memory Verse: "My son if sinners entice you, do not consent." Proverbs 1:10 (NKJV)

Prayer: *O Lord, give me the grace to fix my eyes upon you all the time, in the name of Jesus.*

December 01ˢᵗ

The Word Today: Psalm 67:5-7

".... O God; let all the people praise thee. Then shall the earth yield her increase; and God, even our own God, shall bless us......"

MY HEART-FULL PRAISE SHALL BRING FORTH MY BLESSINGS!

*I*f the Lord had not been on our side when the enemy rose up against us they would have swallowed us up. Saint, praise God today for being your defender, your Protector, the One fighting your battles, worship Him for being your Provider! Praise Him for loving you. You must express your appreciation of His love by praising Him like you've never done before! Praise and worship Him, magnify His Holy name! Show Him that you love Him too with praise. Thank the Lord for accepting your praise in Jesus' name.

PRAISE THUS ALL DAY THIS MONTH:

Father, King of Glory; Ancient of Days, Unchangeable Lord from everlasting to everlasting I will adore and magnify Your Holy Name. You are the Almighty! There's no one like You! My Defender! The Helper of the helpless! In Jesus' name I worship!

DECEMBER BIRTHDAY AND MARRIAGE ANNIVERSARY PRAYERS

Father I commit your children born in December and those celebrating their wedding this month into Your everlasting hand. December is the 12th month of the year, 12 is the number of covenant. Father, I ask that as they begin a new year in their lives, perform every promise You have for them speedily, do something new for them and their loved ones. Give them new joy, new blessings, new breakthroughs and testimonies. Let them serve You to the very end, in Jesus' name. Amen!

December 02nd

The Word Today: Ezekiel 34:23-26

I PROPHECY! THIS IS MY SEASON OF SHOWERS OF BLESSINGS!

The end of the year is usually the period of stock taking; this is the time to evaluate your achievement all through the previous months. It is not a time of major investment if any at all; but a time to assess your current investments. In fact, in many organizations, the end of the year is marked with reduced rate of activity. For many who worked hard and have been blessed by God, it is a season of collating results, rejoicing and enjoying the fruits of their labor; while for those who are less fortunate, it is a period for sober reflections, re-planning and re-strategizing for the forth coming year. I do not know which of the above categories you find yourself, but as long as you are a Believer, I have good news for you. This is your season of showers of blessings, for the Lord will open the windows of heaven and pour you abundant blessings in Jesus' name. Amen!

When the bible talks about showers of blessings, it connotes overflowing blessings. These include divine provision to meet every of your various need: healings, fame, promotion, success etc. The only thing that God needs to release such blessings upon His people is a declaration by His Oracle and the acceptance of the declared word of the recipient by faith. Have you fallen into the depths of debt, depression and melancholy because of constant failures? Now is your season of change. All you have to do is to have faith and accept what God is doing in your life and begin to work joyfully as you receive your shower of blessings in Jesus' name!

Prayer: *This day I step into my shower of blessings!*

195

The Word Today: 1 Kings 3:16-28

LORD! RELEASE THE ANOINTING FOR WISDOM UPON ME!

As a young Believer, I did not see the ingenuity in Solomon's decision to give the child to the woman who said they should allow the disputed child to live. In my estimation then, it was easy for anyone with any amount of intelligence to decipher the truth from that situation. What I did not understand then was the fact that the idea of killing the baby to test the women's claim to the live child was Solomon's. I now do appreciate the wisdom of the King. Surely being faced with two crying women laying claim to one child was a difficult situation. I can imagine in how many different directions Solomon's mind would have gone. Since, he did not have any previous record of such a case.

The logic he used to resolve the issue was really unique. No wonder he was regarded as the wisest man that ever lived. It took an intrinsic analysis and understanding of the originality of the process to convince me that Solomon was really an extra-ordinarily wise man. Further than that, my analysis of the Wisdom of Solomon taught me that wisdom is a gift of God that can be received through many ways including revelation, impartation and association. Having realized all these, I prayed for and by His grace for you to receive the gift of wisdom from God in Jesus' name. It is that gift I seek to impart upon you this day. I don't know whether you desire it or not but if you do, then stretch forth your faith to receive it now. And as you do so, I decree, the anointing for wisdom is released upon you now!

Prayer: *Lord! By faith in Your Word I receive the anointing of wisdom now in the name of Jesus. Amen!*

December 04th

The Word Today: 1 Samuel 18:1-5

THE LORD WILL CHANGE MY ADDRESS FOR GOOD THIS DAY!

*D*avid was a diligent shepherd boy dwelling in Bethlehem until he slew Goliath of Gath in 1 Samuel 17. According to the scriptures, as soon as he presented the head of Goliath to the king, *"Saul took him that day and would let him go no more home to his father's house.... And David went out whithersoever Saul sent him.... And Saul set him over the men of war."*

And so did the residential address of David change from the pasture of Bethlehem to the palace of King Saul where he became a captain. Maybe you have been living in the slum or ghetto all your life thus far and yet have no hope of making a decent living. Maybe you have done odd jobs with minimum wages for years and as yet got no other respectable alternatives that could change your status. Or you may have been at the lower rung of the ladder in your career without clear signs of prospect of any promotion and progress.

Saint! Hear the word of the living God! This day your address is changing for good in the name of Jesus. Amen! The same God, who made room at the top for David, has remembered you for divine elevation this day in the name of Jesus. Amen! By the end of this month, something positively radical will happen in your life to provoke divine intervention in your situation in Jesus' name. Amen! The Lord God will remember you for divine promotion and exaltation in Jesus' name. Amen!

Prayer: *O Lord! Grant unto me the grace for divine elevation to change my situation in the name of Jesus. Amen!*

197

December 05th

The Word Today: Philippians 4:19

"But my God shall supply all your need according to his riches in glory by Christ Jesus."

I DECREE! I SHALL NOT LACK ANY GOOD THING!

If Believers really understand the implication of Philippians 4:19 then, there will be no lack in the Christendom. That verse is simply saying that God is the bank that never fails. Imagine what it would be like to have the biggest bank in the world as your partner. That would mean; no business or contract proposal would be too big for you because you have the vault of a great bank as your support. The implication is that everybody and organization would seek to do business with you. You can't lack. So, how can you then lack, when you have God the owner of the universe as your support. Psalm 24:1.

The reason some Christians do suffer lack is because they operate in the hard work consciousness level instead of the prosperity consciousness level because of lack of knowledge. Hard work is good but the hardest workers are not the wealthiest. The wealthiest people are those who even though they work hard, know and operate at the spiritual realm of prosperity. By this I mean, those who realizes that what they get in the physical is a product of what they create in the spiritual. Jacob was such a man. He created the wealth he needed in the spiritual even against the physical manipulations of Laban his father in-law Genesis 30. Do you desire wealth? Learn to tap into wealth in the spirit realm. If you can really visualize it you can get it. I prophesy you won't lack henceforth in Jesus' name.

Prayer: *I command the wealth consciousness of Jacob to rest upon me now in Jesus' name. Amen!*

WORD SWORD OF THE ORACLE

The Word Today: Leviticus 1:5 (NKJV)

*"He shall kill the bull before the Lord; and the **priests,** Aaron's sons, shall bring the blood and sprinkle the blood all around on the altar that is by the door of the tabernacle of meeting."*

PRIEST [HEBREW] *KOHEN*

The English word Priest is *Kohen* in the Hebrew Language as used in Leviticus 1:5, Leviticus 6:6, Leviticus 27:21, 2 Chronicles 35:2 Strong's #3548. The Priesthood was not unique to the Israelites. From the Egyptians to the Philistines, all the ancient Middle Eastern nations had a class of priest. At Mount Sinai, God consecrated Aaron and his descendants as priests Exodus 28:1. They were to be representative of the people before God, offering sacrifices and prayers on their behalf. Furthermore they instructed the people about their religious duties and the character of God Deuteronomy 33:8-10. One of the foundational principles of the Israelite covenant with God at Sinai was that, the nation as a whole would become "a kingdom of priests" Exodus 19:6. There have been many proposed interpretations of this expression. Exodus 19:5 Exodus 19:6.

The New Testament describes Jesus Christ as our High Priest Hebrews 5:10. Through His death on the Cross, the formal priesthood was abolished Hebrews 10:11-12. In its stead, all believers become priest not to offer animal sacrifices but to pray, worship and witness to others about Jesus Hebrews 13:15-16, 1 Peter 2:5, 1 Peter 2:9 and Revelation 1:5-6.

Prayer: *Lord! Empower me to be effective at my priestly duties!*

CHURCH AND HOME SUNDAY SCHOOL

THE EIGHTH COMMANDMENT

WHAT IS THE EIGHTH COMMANDMENT?

"You shall not steal." Exodus 20:15 (NKJV)

WHAT ARE WE COMMANDED BY THE EIGHT COMMANDMENT?

We are to respect the property of others, to pay our debts, live up to business agreements and to be honest in all our dealings.

WHAT IS FORBIDDEN BY THE EIGHTH COMMANDMENT?

1) All kind of theft and fraud, as well as sinful longing for anything that belongs to our neighbors.

"Let him who stole steal no longer, but rather let him labor, working with his hands what is good, that he may have something to give him who has need." Ephesians 4:28 (NKJV)

"Woe to him who builds his house by unrighteousness; and his chambers by injustice, who uses his neighbor's service without wages, and gives him nothing for his work." Jeremiah 22:13.

"For even when we were with you, we commanded you this: If anyone will not work, neither shall he eat." 2 Thessalonians 3:10

2) Cheating, false reporting for income tax returns, damaging or buying stolen property, is forbidden by the eighth commandment and the Word of God.

"You shall do no injustice in judgment, in measurement of length, weight, or volume." Leviticus 19:35 (NKJV)

"The wicked borrows and does not repay, but the righteous shows mercy and gives." Psalm 37:21 (NKJV)

"Whoever is a partner with a thief hates his own life; He swears to tell the truth, but reveals nothing." Proverbs 29:24 (NKJV)

WHAT DOES GOD REQUIRE OF US IN THE EIGHTH COMMANDMENT?

God requires us to:

1) Respect the property of our neighbors:

"If you meet your enemy's ox or his donkey going astray, you shall surely bring it back to him again." Exodus 23:4 (NKJV)

"Therefore, whatever you want men to do to you, do also to them, for this is the Law and the Prophets." Matthew 7:12

2) Help our neighbor whenever we can:

"Give to him who asks you, and from him who wants to borrow from you do not turn away." Matthew 5:42 (NKJV)

"He who has pity on the poor lends to the Lord, and He will pay back what he has given." Proverbs 19:17 (NKJV)

"But do not forget to do good and to share, for with such sacrifices God is well pleased." Hebrews 13:16 (NKJV)

3) Rejoice when we see our neighbors prosper:

"Love suffers long and is kind; love does not envy; love does not parade itself, is not puffed up; does not behave rudely, does not seek its own, is not provoked, thinks no evil." 1 Corinthians 13:4-5.

SUNDAY SCHOOL QUESTIONS

Q1. WHAT IS THE EIGHTH COMMANDMENT? Q2. WHAT ARE WE COMMANDED BY THE EIGHT COMMANDMENT?
Q3. WHAT IS FORBIDDEN BY THE EIGHTH COMMANDMENT?   Q4. WHAT DOES GOD REQUIRE OF US IN THE EIGHTH COMMANDMENT?

> **Memory Verse:** Exodus 20:15 (NKJV) *"You shall not steal."*

Today's Prayer

1. *Lord! Take away from me the spirit of covetousness in the name of Jesus. Amen!*
2. *Lord! Deliver me from envy and jealousy in Jesus' name.*
3. *O God! Destroy the spirit of greed and selfishness in me!*
4. *Father! Give me the grace to pay restitution to anyone I have stolen from knowingly and or unknowingly!*
5. *Oh Lord, released a terrifying noise to chase out evil tenants in my life in the name of Jesus.*
6. *My progress, I command you now rise up without hindrance in Jesus' name.*
7. *Every spiritual robber in my life, receive thunder and scatter in the name of Jesus. Amen!*
8. *Every witchcraft cage in my life, break in Jesus' name.*
9. *You crown of non-achievement on my head, roast to ashes in the name of Jesus. Amen!*
10. *Thank You Father! For Your Love! Thank You Holy Spirit!*
11. *Thank You Lord Jesus for prayer answered!*

THE LORD GOD SHALL PERFECT ALL THAT CONCERNS ME!

*A*re you going through difficulties? Are the pressures of life pushing you around? Have you wondered for too long when the storms of life that are pushing you around would not cease to exist and continue? Saint! Hear the word of God! The Lord will perfect that which concerns you in due time in Jesus' name!

When the bible says a thousand years in the eyes of men is like a day with God, it is referring to such delay you are dealing with now. The Lord is a perfect planner. He will not send divine intervention too earlier or too late, He is always on time. There is no situation He is not aware of; no circumstance can catch Him unawares. Nothing is beyond His control; He has absolute control of all situations. God's way is higher than ours, when we expect Him to intervene might not be the best time for us. With hindsight, Lazarus and his sisters appreciated Jesus for turning him into a celebrity by raising him from the dead. John 11. But when Lazarus lay on the death bed, they did not feel that way though. They were offended by the inability of Jesus to come much earlier to their rescue. But had Jesus heeded their call, healing Lazarus would have simply been just one of the others. God's plan was to make the testimony of Lazarus an eternal reference point in the history of Christianity. So, when His timing was right, He showed up. Saint! Whatever unpleasant situation you are dealing with right now I want you to know that it is still under the control of the almighty God. Are you anxious? Relax for God will help you in Jesus' name!

Prayer: *Lord! I commit all my issues into your hand, perfect all that concerns me in Jesus' name. Amen!*

The Word Today: Proverbs 21:1

GOD WILL TURN THE HEART OF PEOPLE TO FAVOR ME!

The above passage is simply saying that God is the ultimate decider in the affairs of men. He is the ultimate sovereign power and nothing happens without His consent. Even though, God allows man the freedom of choice, He reserves the right to veto, direct and or orchestrate a person's thought process towards certain direction. Esther understood this principle. That is why she directed the Jews in Susan to fast and pray along with her before going to the king uninvited in Esther Chapter 5. She knew that God can influence the King to favor her. The expected death sentence for the breach of protocol was changed to an open check. Your open check from God is next in Jesus' name!

Is your fate and faith hanging on the balance because you are waiting for those in authority to make a decision concerning you? Saint! I want you to know that your fate is not in the hand of anyone but God's. So, instead of sending emissaries or making overtures to that person[s], you can pray to God to change their disposition to favor you. When you do so, you have influenced that situation from the source. Anything that is changed from the source is automatically changed all over. As you meet people daily, there are three things that may happen. They may either, favor, disfavor or be indifference to you. A prevalence of the first option brings good success while the others bring failure and stagnation respectively. I now prophesy, God will turn the hearts of people in your favor in Jesus' name. Amen!

Prayer: *Father Lord! Turn the heart of people in my favor in Jesus' name. Amen!*

December 10th

The Word Today: 2 Chronicles 32:27-33

"...He prospered in all his works (2 Chr. 32:30) *... and all Judah and the inhabitants of Jerusalem did him honored at his death* (2 Chr. 32:33)."*

THE LORD GOD SHALL EXCEEDINGLY BLESS AND HONOR ME!

In the above scriptures, in spite of the adversary of Hezekiah, he *"....had exceeding much riches and honor; for God had given him substance very much; And Hezekiah prospered in all his works and all Judah and the inhabitants of Jerusalem did him honor at his death."* I prophesy the Lord to exceedingly bless you with riches and honor, the Lord to give you much substance and prosper you in all your works even unto death as He did with Hezekiah in Jesus' mighty name. Amen! God made you an undefeated and undefeatable World Champion. Romans 8:37 says you are more than conquerors because He that is in you is greater than your adversaries that is in this world, there may be many battles for you to fight, but you will win them all. Psalm 34:19 says *"many are the afflictions of the righteous but the Lord delivered him from them all."* You shall be delivered too!

In Isaiah 54:17, God said there's no weapon fashioned against you that will prosper! In Deuteronomy 28:7, He said all the enemies that rise up against you shall be smitten before your face. This month God will fight for you. Every enemy that comes against you one way, they shall scatter in seven ways in Jesus' name. Amen! Every divination, every enchantment and negative pronouncement against you will not come to pass and they shall not stand in Jesus' name. Amen! Numbers 23:23, Isaiah 8:9-10.

Prayer: *Oh God of Hezekiah give me great substance, riches, and proper me physically and spiritually all the days of my life!*

205

The Word Today: 2 Chronicles 32:27-33

"And Hezekiah had exceeding much riches and honor...... for God had given him substance very much....." 2 Chronicles 32:27 &29

I DECLARE! I SHALL PREVIAL IN ALL MAY BATTLES!

"And He prospered in all his works 2 Chronicles 32:30

"... and all Judah and the inhabitants of Jerusalem did him honor at his death." 2 Chronicles 32:33.

What an account! Hezekiah had it all in life. He won all his battles and saw the end of his enemies. He was very rich and favored in his lifetime. Even in death men honored him. What more can a man want? I prophesy, like Hezekiah, you shall enjoy all the good things of life and even in death men shall continually honor you in Jesus' name. Amen!

Hezekiah's heritage can be yours. In fact, by the covenant of the blood of Jesus Christ, it has been made much easier for you. All you have to do is to know it. Believe it, claim it for yourself, start confessing it to posses it and then work towards it. As you do so, I prophesy favorable situations will begin to fall in place for you and you shall have exceeding great riches and honor in your lifetime as you win all your battles in Jesus' name. Amen!

This week, you shall see a favorable sign that will lead you onto your breakthrough in Jesus' mighty name Amen!

Prayer: *O God! By Your Power! Henceforth, I shall prosper in all the works of my hand. I declare total victory in all my battles in Jesus' name. Amen!*

I AM DELIVERED FROM ALL INFIRMITY AND AFFLICTIONS!

"When I joined the Oracle of God international Ministries about a year ago, I was head over heel with tons of issues. I wondered if the God of the Oracle could heal me of the hypertension and diabetes that had afflicted me for years; among other health complications, financial and marital issues. In the course of looking for solution to my problems, I had prayed, cried and visited several places to seek help: Churches, prayer houses, hospitals, orthodox and unorthodox medications and other places I am not so proud of, to no avail. Nevertheless, after years of no result, I quit trying and accepted my situation and continued taking one prescription drug to another; I became a junky, an addict indeed. Then a friend of one of my siblings' invited me to the grant opening of the Indian Head campus of the Oracle of God International Ministries in Maryland USA. And Prophet Stevie prayed for me and declared that the infirmity and afflictions in my life is over in the name of Jesus. True to the word of the Oracle of God, when I went to the hospital my doctor was awed at my healing and took me out of the medications. I give God all the glory! Alleluia!" Sister Z.

Do you appreciate the above praise report? Do you believe that the same God of the Oracle can do the same for you? If you do, I declare your deliverance from whatever infirmity or affliction that you or your loved ones are dealing with right now in Jesus' name! Respite is coming for you in Jesus' name. Amen!

Prayer: *O God! Deliver me from all my infirmity and afflictions in the name of Jesus. Amen!*

WORD SWORD OF THE ORACLE

The Word Today: Leviticus 1:4 (NKJV)

---

*" Then he shall put his hand on the head of the burnt offering, and it will be accepted on his behalf to make **atonement** for him."*

ATONEMENT [HEBREW] *KAPHAR*

The word atonement, *Kaphar* in Hebrew as used in Leviticus 1:4, Leviticus 9:7, Leviticus 14:18 and 2 Samuel 21:3 Strong's #3722: has various uses and meanings it could mean "to cover", "to appease", "to ransom." In the Scriptures it more commonly speaks of payment for sin. All of the various offerings in the Jewish sacrificial system are described as effecting atonement. The key idea is that these offerings gained the favor of God, and God removed the worshipper's guilt. The sacrifice was presented as a substitute for the life of the offender's sin and turned aside God's wrath. Like the Lambs offered to atone for the sins of the Israelites, Jesus' life was offered as a substitute for ours. His death turned away God's wrath and atoned for our own sins Romans 3:25.

At the very heart of the Christian belief system lays this all-important doctrine of the Atonement. The Apostle Paul, himself an advocate of "sound doctrine," in a condensed statement of what the Christian Church believes, said, *"For I delivered unto you first of all that which I also received, how that Christ died for our sins according to the Scriptures; and that He was buried, and that He rose again the third day according to the Scriptures."* 1 Corinthians 15:3-4. Some religious leaders object vigorously to the "Doctrine of the Atonement" that the Death of Jesus Christ was sacrificial and necessary for man's redemption; but we must proceed on this sound biblical doctrine to pursue and continue with it no matter what.

CHURCH AND HOME SUNDAY SCHOOL

THE NINTH COMMANDMENT

WHAT IS THE NINETH COMMANDMENT?

"You shall not bear false witness against your neighbor." Exodus 20:16 (NKJV)

WHAT ARE WE COMMANDED BY THE NINTH COMMANDMENT?

We are commanded to be truthful in all things, especially in matters that concern the good name or honor of our neighbor.

WHAT DOES GOD FORBID IN THE NINETH COMMANDMENT?

God forbids us to judge others, He forbids us to lie, to make rash judgments, to commit slander, detraction, perjury, or to reveal secrets about another's character.

"Let none of you think evil in your heart against your neighbor; and do not love a false oath. For all these are things that I hate,' Says the Lord." Zechariah 8:17 (NKJV)

"Moreover if your brother sins against you, go and tell him his fault between you and him alone. If he hears you, you have gained your brother." Matthew 18:15 (NKJV)

WHAT IS THE SIN OF DETRACTION?

The sin of detraction is making known the hidden faults of another without a good reason.

"A talebearer reveals secrets, but he who is of a faithful spirit conceals a matter." Proverbs 11:13 (NKJV)

WHAT IS THE SIN OF SLANDER?

The sin of slander is a deliberate lying to injure the good name of another person.

"Do not speak evil of one another, brethren. He who speaks evil of a brother and judges his brother, speaks evil of the law and judges the law. But if you judge the law, you are not a doer of the law but a judge." James 4:11 (NKJV)

"You give your mouth to evil, and your tongue frames deceit. You sit and speak against your brother; you slander your own mother's son. These things you have done, and I kept silent; You thought that I was altogether like you; but I will rebuke you, and set them in order before your eyes. "Now consider this, you who forget God, lest I tear you in pieces, and there be none to deliver:" Psalm 50:19-22 (NKJV)

SUNDAY SCHOOL QUESTIONS

Q1. WHAT IS THE NINETH COMMANDMENT?
Q2. WHAT ARE WE COMMANDED BY THE NINETH COMMANDMENT?
Q3. WHAT DOES GOD FORBID IN THE NINETH COMMANDMENT?
Q4. WHAT IS THE SIN OF DETRACTION?
Q5. WHAT IS THE SIN OF SLANDER?

> **Memory Verse:** "You shall not bear false witness against your neighbor." Exodus 20:16 (NKJV)

Prayer: *Lord forgive all my sins against my neighbors.*

The Word Today: 1 Samuel 11:1-2 (The Message)

"...... Nahash said, "I'll make a treaty with you on one condition: that every right eye among you be gouged out....."

I PROPHESY! MY DELIVERANCE FROM THE NAHASH OF LIFE!

God's people ceded their dominion to the enemy by asking for a truce in Gilead. Emboldened by the obvious show of weakness, Nahash whose name means 'magnificent snake' insisted that he would have them remove their right eyes as a condition for the truce. Nahash' position connotes everlasting threatening for the Gileadites. In biblical days, warriors covered the left side of their faces with their shields, while they fought with their spears in their right hands. So if they had their right eyes thrust out, the men of Gilead could no longer fight. So, Nahash' plan was to completely cripple the army of Gilead and put them in permanent servitude.

In today's terms, Nahash represents powers that insist on putting Believers in perpetual slavery and struggle, powers that places you in categories and compartments. But by the Spirit of the Lord, as the Oracle of God I come to bring you out of that compartment in Jesus' name. Amen! Some of these powers use crafty schemes like false promises of healings, wealth, and provisional peace etc., to put the people of God in bondage. Some cling onto legal grounds presented by ignorant ancestors while some others use intimidation and fear to humiliate their victim. Is any Nahash holding you captive? I prophesy the Lord shall deliver you from the Nahash of your life in Jesus' name.

Prayer: *I crush every Nahash that is tormenting my life in Jesus' name. Amen!*

I PROPHESY! GOD SHALL AFFLICT THOSE THAT ARE AGAINST ME!

In the scriptures, many people suffer afflictions because they place themselves against God's children. Nabal was smitten to death in 1 Samuel 25:38. Others were struck with different kinds of infirmities: insanity- Daniel 4:28-33, Blindness- Acts 9:1-5, Leprosy- 2 Kings 5:25-27 etc. Bar-Jesus, the subject of our word today, was one of such people too. For making himself a hindrance to the gospel, he was afflicted with blindness by the decree of Apostle Paul. Anyone who is in the way of God's children is courting trouble, because the Saints are representatives of God on earth. Just like anyone that attacks the ambassador of a country in a foreign land seeks trouble with the nation, anyone who decides to trouble you will definitely receive double trouble at the hands of the almighty God.

Are you a right standing born again Believer? Then know that you are untouchable. As a Believer in good standing with God, you belong to the army of the living God. So, just like Goliath was disgraced for defying and reproaching the army of the living God, anybody who defies you shall be disgraced. Are there people who have persistently put themselves against you to frustrate you? Are there members of your family perpetrating household wickedness against you? Is there anyone, anywhere reveling themselves in ridiculing you because of your faith? Is it work place wickedness? I decree the wrath of God upon them now in Jesus' name. Amen!

Prayer: *I invoke the wrath of God upon my adversaries in Jesus' name. Amen!*

I PROPHESY! MY PROBLEM SHALL LINK ME TO MY MIRACLE!

For refusing to sleep with his master's wife, Joseph was removed from his position as Portiphar's overseer and thrown into jail in Genesis 39. No sooner had he settled in prison than the Lord came to him and divinely arranged his meetings with the butler who later recommended him to Pharaoh in Genesis 41:9-13. So, what the enemy meant for evil became the link to Joseph's miracle. So, what Joseph lost to the enemy earlier on, proved insignificant compared to what he gained later.

You may have been previously rich or wealthy, but you are now wallowing in abject poverty. You may have lost relevance in your office or in society because you refused to engage in fraud, bribery and corruption. Or maybe you have been seeking God's face because of gang-up of retrogressive forces against you. Brethren, I declare in the name of Jesus Christ that the challenge you are facing today will connect you to your miracle in the name of Jesus. Amen!

The God of Joseph, has sent me to declare unto you that He is about to use the situation you are facing right now to elevate you beyond your wildest dream in the name of Jesus. Better believe it, for you need to believe it to receive it and start confessing what you believe, for that will lead to your possess it. Whatsoever evil the enemy meant for you will soon become the link to your miracle because God has visited you today by grace!

Prayer: *My problems shall connect me to my miracle in Jesus' name. Amen!*

December 18th

The Word Today: Exodus 19:1-5 (NKJV)

"...Now therefore, if you will indeed obey My voice and keep My covenant, then you shall be a special treasure to Me above all people; for all the earth is Mine."

I DECLARE! I AM A PECULIAR TREASURE TO THE LORD GOD!

When you love a person, it is only natural to always wish that person well. People are over-protective of their loved ones. The reason is that by nature, love evokes emotions of attachment and gentleness. So as humans when we love; our loved ones become a special part of our feelings and emotions. This is pretty much the same with God. When He loves you, you become an integral part of Him and His responsibility. When He chooses you as His peculiar treasure you begin to enjoy spectacular favor. The children of God were honored with such a position of priority. They became a special people in God scheme of things, because of the covenant of God with their fathers. Consequently, God in His infinite wisdom decided to destroy seven kingdoms in order to establish Israel. I prophesy you are a peculiar treasure unto God, in Jesus' name. Amen!

Brethren! When you become a peculiar treasure to God, you become a special candidate for uncommon favors, unusual breakthroughs and great mercies, your failures would be replaced with successes. Divine favor will remove the struggle in your life. You will begin to receive without asking. Do you desire such blessings? If so; declare the following prayer and confession severally in Jesus' powerful name.

Prayer: *I am a special person in the eyes of God. Therefore, He is watching over me to ensure that I am forever blessed!*

214

The Word Today: John 17:15-20

I DECREE! MY DELIVERANCE FROM ALL EVIL!

When Jesus prayed for His disciples, in our text passage above, He gave the blueprint of the caring nature of God. He showed that He is interested in the well being of His people. God is actually interested in your well-being. As proof of His interest, Jesus extended the prayer to include you.

2 Chronicles 16:9 says *"for the eyes of the LORD run to and fro throughout the whole earth, to shew himself strong on behalf of them whose heart is perfect toward him...."*

God wants to strengthen your resolve, He wants you to know that He is mighty to save and He will show Himself strong on your behalf, He wants you to trust His might. As a result, God's eyes are on you. And if God's eyes are on you, then you can be rest assured that as He did for the apostles in the post -Christ era He will do for you, He will protect you from all evil in Jesus' name!

Are you afraid of proclaiming your faith for fear of attacks from family and friends? Be not afraid for He that is in you is greater than they that are in the world. Saint, I say again, fear not for the Lord is with you. Do not live your life in fear. Take bold a decision today; take bold a step that would take you into your breakthrough without fear. As soon as you seek and get divine direction, take that bold step; declare your faith, take that career decision, go into that business. Fear is a snare, don't get ensnared by fear. Step into your destiny now as I prophesy unto you this day God shall keep you from all evil in Jesus' name!

Prayer: *I soak myself in the blood of Jesus. As a sign of His covenant with me, God shall keep me from evil in Jesus' name!*

215

WORD SWORD OF THE ORACLE

The Word Today: Leviticus 16:16 (NKJV)

*"So he shall make atonement for the Holy Place, because of the uncleanness of the children of Israel, and because of their **transgressions,** for all their sins; and so he shall do for the tabernacle of meeting which remains among them in the midst of their uncleanness."*

TRANSGRESSIONS [HEBREW] *PESHA'*

The Hebrew word *Pasha* in Lev. 16:16, Lev. 16:21, Ps. 32:1, Ps. 32:5 Strong's #6588 means "to revolt" 2 Kings 8:20, "to offend" Prov. 18:19, "to rebel or to transgress" in the sense of crossing boundary Jer. 3:13; is violating God's Law as revealed to Moses. In other words, someone crossing the limits that God had established. To "transgress," is to pass over or go beyond; to overpass, as any rule prescribed as the limit of duty; to break or violate, as a law, civil or moral; the act of transgressing; the violation of a law or known principle of rectitude; breach of command; offense; crime and sin. In the Old Testament *pasha'*, occurs 80 times, rendered in all versions as "transgression." It means "rebellion". The word "rebellion" differs in that it may be in the heart, though no opportunity should be granted for its manifestation: Prov. 17:11. The New Testament uses the Latin word *parabasis,* "trespass": "The law was added because of transgressions" Gal. 3:19, Rom. 4:15, Heb. 9:15. Although rebelling against God was a grave mistake, God made provision for Israel's transgressions in the Day of Atonement Lev. 16:15-19. The priest could make atonement for Israel's sin, and the nation could be reconciled to God. Like ancient Israel, we are in rebellion against God. In fact, it was "our transgressions" that wounded Jesus Christ Isaiah 53:5-8, 1 Peter 2:24.

CHURCH AND HOME SUNDAY SCHOOL

WHAT IS PERJURY?

Perjury is the willful telling of lies, against our neighbor, while under oath in a court of law.

"A false witness will not go unpunished, and he who speaks lies will not escape." Proverbs 19:5 (NKJV)

BIBLE NARRATIVES:

1) FALSE WITNESSES TESTIFIED AGAINST JESUS CHRIST: MATTHEW 26:59-61
2) FALSE WITNESSES AROSE AGAINST NABOTH: 1 KINGS 21:13

WHAT KIND OF LYING IS ESPECIALLY FORBIDDEN BY THE NINETH COMMANDMENT?

Jesus said, *"I am... the truth..."* in John 14:6 and in the ninth commandment God tells us to love truth and show love for others by respecting their reputation. The word of God especially forbids us to lie about our neighbor or to lie to our neighbor.

"Therefore, putting away lying, "Let each one of you speak truth with his neighbor," for we are members of one another." Ephesians 4:25 (NKJV)

WHEN ARE WE OBLIGATED TO KEEP SOMETHING SECRET?

When we have promise not to reveal a secret, when something is told us in confidence, or when the good of another is at stake.

WHY ARE WE FORBIDDEN TO JUDGE OTHERS?

$\mathscr{We}$ are forbidden to judge others because God has command it and He will pardon us only as we pardon those who have offended us.

"Judge not, and you shall not be judged. Condemn not, and you shall not be condemned. Forgive, and you will be forgiven." Luke 6:37 (NKJV)

WHAT DOES GOD REQUIRE OF US IN THE NINTH COMMANDMENT?

God require us to:

1) Defend our neighbor that is to take his part and shield him against false accusations.

"Open your mouth for the speechless, in the cause of all who are appointed to die. Open your mouth, judge righteously, and plead the cause of the poor and needy." Proverbs 31:8-9 (NKJV)

2) Speak well of our neighbor, that is, praise his good qualities and deeds so far as it can be done in keeping with truth.

3) Cover up faults of our neighbor and explain in his favor whatever can be explained.

"And above all things have fervent love for one another, for "love will cover a multitude of sins." 1 Peter 4:8 (NKJV)

"Love bears up under anything and everything that comes, is ever ready to believe the best of every person, its hopes are fadeless under all circumstances, and it endures everything [without weakening]." 1 Corinthians 13:7 (AMP)

SUNDAY SCHOOL QUESTIONS

Q1. WHAT IS PERJURY?
Q2. WHAT KIND OF LYING IS ESPECIALLY FORBIDDEN BY THE NINETH COMMANDMENT?
Q3. WHEN ARE WE OBLIGATED TO KEEP SOMETHING SECRET? Q4. WHY ARE WE FORBIDDEN TO JUDGE OTHERS? Q5. WHAT DOES GOD REQUIRE OF US IN THE NINTH COMMANDMENT?

> **Memory Verse:** "A false witness will not go unpunished, and He who speaks lies will not escape."
> Proverbs 19:5 (NKJV)

Today's Prayers

1. Lord forgive me of any false witness that have bared against anyone in Jesus' name!
2. I forgive anyone that has bared false witness against me in Jesus' gracious name. Amen!
3. Let frustration and disappointment, be the portion of every object fashioned against my life and family.
4. Every tie to polluted objects and items between my life and family, break, in the name of Jesus. Amen!
5. Every unspoken curse against my life, break by fire!
6. Every curse pronounced inwardly against my destiny, break, in the name of Jesus. Amen!
7. Inward curses, militating against my virtues, break!
8. Any power given the mandate to curse and hinder your progress, summersault and die, in Jesus' name.
9. Thank God in advance for answered prayers!

"... and his own counsel shall cast him down. For he is cast into a net by his own feet and he walketh upon a snare".

I DECREE AND DECLARE! MY PURSURERS SHALL WALK INTO A SNARE!

The American Vietnam War of the late sixties is one war the United States of America cannot forget in a hurry. The reason is that they lost countless soldiers in that war and left Vietnam with shame faced. In fact, up till today, it has remained a mystery how the tiny nation of Vietnam could withstand and humble the US with her huge military machines and resources.

A profound scrutiny of the tactics employed by the Vietnamese army is the divine principle of ensnaring ones opponents. Aware of the huge differences in their military might, the Vietnamese knew they could never stand up to the Americans in a head to head war. So, they resorted to a system of leading the enemy into booby traps, which they had set in remote bushes. This system was so effective that within a short while the American contingent lost so many soldiers that there was a large outcry for the country to withdraw from Vietnam. Consequently, America left Vietnam humiliated. Every physical manifestation is a creation of the spiritual. So, there are spiritual booby traps according to Job 18:8 the wicked is cast into a net by his own feet. So, I prophesy, your pursuers shall walk into a snare in Jesus' name. Amen!

Prayer: *Today, I weave a trap around every pursuer of my destiny, I command them to walk into a snare and be destroyed in Jesus' name. Amen!*

I KNOW! MY HELP SHALL COME FROM THE LORD MY GOD!

*S*aint! Where do you seek help when you are in need? Are you one of those who are here today and there the next day? Are you in the house of God on Sunday morning and in the occult and herbalist house the next evening? Beloved, there is no help anywhere else than from God through Jesus Christ. Sometimes, there is need for man to seek help when situations of life are beyond control. In such case, some people go to man for directions. Worse still some go to places that are ungodly. Such places are what our text-verse above referred to as Egypt. Those who do so, run the risk of evoking the wrath of God upon them, because, they misplaced their trust by placing their faith in man. If you are one of such people, there is still chance for you to reprieve today if you retrace your steps and look up to God. Psalm 121 says the help of man should come from above. So, at each point that you are in a crossroad, cross over to God; there is need for you to look up to you maker. God's love for man is ever flowing; He is always looking at you to accord you the desired recognition. If you know how to do that, you will always get help from God.

That was the difference between David and Saul. Whereas David always looked up to God for help, Saul consulted witches and mediums for direction. So Saul's kingdom was cut short and David's became everlasting. Saint! Where is your focus? I admonish you this day, direct it to the God of David and it shall be well with you without doubt in Jesus' name. Amen!

Prayer: *Lord! Help me victoriously as I look up to You!*

221

December 24ᵗʰ

The Word Today: Mark 10:46-52

"...And when he heard that it was Jesus of Nazareth, he began to cry out and say, "Jesus, Son of David, have mercy on me!" Then many warned him to be quiet; but he cried out all the more, "Son of David, have mercy on me!" So Jesus stood still and commanded him to be called. Then they called the blind man, saying to him, "Be of good cheer. Rise, He is calling you."

I KNOW! CHRIST JESUS SHALL RESPOND TO MY CRIES!

A long time ago, I came to the conclusion that the worst misfortune that can befall a man is blindness. Try walking around with your eyes close for a while and you will appreciate sight. It is so limiting and difficult, so frustrating and almost suffocating. Indeed blindness is about the worst affliction that can be. If that is the case and you agree, then Blind Bartimaeus must have been a very bitter man. He must have cried on countless occasions because of his condition. But a day came when his cry drew the attention of Jesus Christ the son of David. That ended his aguish. I decree an end to your own aguish this day in the name of Jesus. Amen!

I do not know what the enemy has afflicted you with. But I tell you that the end of this year also mark the end of your afflictions in the name of Jesus. Amen! Just like sorrow came to an end for Bartimaeus as soon as Jesus stepped into his situation, the end has come for your cries and sorrows in Jesus' name. Amen!

Prayer: Lord Jesus! Son of David have mercy on me and deliver me from the darkness of my life in Jesus' name. Amen!

The Word Today: Numbers 23:13-23

I DECLARE! THERE SHALL BE NO ENCHANTMENT AGAINST ME!

Years ago a young man narrated his ordeal to me. He was a banker with a major development bank. According to him, periodically, he loses money that is put in his charge in strange circumstances, even his own personal funds were disappearing. Severally in the past he's lost petty sums of money and jewelry. But recently the amount and sum of money disappearing is staggering and much more frequently too. The plight of this man is a classic case of bewitchment. The man was under enchantment and divination. Literally, enchantment is a pronounced curse or imprecation against a person, to bring upon such victim a magical or witchcraft spell and jinx. When a person is under such enchantment he or she attracts evil without cause or knowing why. This makes the person a perfect victim.

An enchantment is like a curse. It brings negative aura or energy around a victim and makes him or her susceptible to disasters. For some people it puts them under a curse of hatred. Wherever they go, people just hate them. Consequently, in place of acceptance, help and love, they are rejected, detested and attacked. Balak, King of Moab understood the implications of enchantment. That is why he hired Balaam to place a curse on the Israelites. But because the seal of the Lord was upon them, they could not be cursed. Right now I place the seal of God upon you in Jesus' name. And so, there shall be no divination and enchantment against you!

Prayer: *I break every curse upon me now in Jesus' name. Amen!*

223

December 26th

The Word Today: 2 Samuel 6:8-10

I DECREE AND DECLARE! I SHALL NOT BE MARKED FOR MISFORTUNE!

𝒞an you imagine? Because King David does not want to die, the Ark of God that just killed Uzzah for coming in contact with it was to be sent to the house of Obed-Edom. The king who should have custody of the Ark of God rejected it and decide to send it to the house of Obed-Edom. By implication David uses Obed-Edom as a guinea pig [experimental material]. He wished to see from its reaction to Obed-Edom whether God through the ark, wish to destroy the people. Obed-Edom was expendable. You shall not be in the name of Jesus. Amen!

As far as King David is concern, if the ark was commissioned for disaster, the best or first person that should die is Obed-Edom. What a fate! Some people are like Obed-Edom. They are disaster and misfortune prone. When misfortune comes to town, their families are sure to be the first to grab it. Disaster just seeks them out of hiding. If you are one of such people, I cancel that destiny of disaster now in the name of Jesus. Amen! For Obed-Edom, his name attracted the misfortune for it meant hated slave. So, he had the worst kind of destiny ahead of him because of the name he bore. Are you one of such people whose destiny has been embargoed because of your first, middle or last name? I cancel every negative effect of your name upon your person and destiny now in Jesus' name! Now, you are marked for favor and fortune in Jesus' name. Amen!

Prayer: *O Lord My God! Separate me from every mark of misfortune in the name of Jesus. Amen!*

224

WORD SWORD OF THE ORACLE

The Word Today: Leviticus 19:30 (NKJV)

"You shall keep My Sabbaths and reverence My sanctuary: I am the Lord."

SANCTUARY [HEBREW] *MIQDASH*

The Hebrew noun Miqdash as used in Lev. 19:30, Ex. 15:17, Ex. 25:8 etc. Strong's #4720: means "holy place" a place separated and dedicated to God. It was the place where God has chosen to meet with His people the Israelites. The priests would atone for their sin; in turn, the people would offer their worship and praise therein. Because it was God's dwelling place, the priests were prohibited from defiling it by entering while they were ceremonially unclean Lev. 21:12. But most important, is that the Israelites had to respect the sanctuary by approaching it with a contrite heart and a determination to praise their creator. Just as Moses had to respect the ground where God made His presence known in Ex. 3:5, so now the Israelites had to respect the place where God had chosen to meet them.

The word sanctuary is derived from the Latin word *sanctuarium.* Sanctity, Sanction and Saint are all from the same root word; and mean a place or person that is set apart as a refuge from danger or hardship. The two Hebrew words of the O. Testament that have been translated as Sanctuary are pronounced *mik-dawsh,* meaning a consecrated place or thing, and *koh-desh,* meaning pure or sacred. In the New T., the Greek word translated as Sanctuary is pronounced *hag-ee-on,* meaning sacred, or holy. Sanctuary in the Bible is also used in reference to the Tabernacle or the Temple; it also was applied to the Promised Land itself, as well as God's Sanctuary in heaven.

225

4ᵗʰ Sunday of the Month of December

CHURCH AND HOME SUNDAY SCHOOL

THE TENTH COMMANDMENT

WHAT IS THE TENTH COMMANDMENT?

"You shall not covet your neighbor's house; you shall not covet your neighbor's wife, nor his male servant, nor his female servant, nor his ox, nor his donkey, nor anything that is your neighbor's." Exodus 20:17 (NKJV)

WHAT DOES COVET MEAN?

To covet means to desire or long for something so strongly that a feeling of discontentment overcomes us. This is usually accompanied by ill will at seeing another's superiority, prosperity or advantage of success. It is a gross form of selfishness that is highly offensive to God.

"And He said to them, "Take heed and beware of covetousness, for one's life does not consist in the abundance of the things he possesses." Then He spoke a parable to them, saying: "The ground of a certain rich man yielded plentifully. And he thought within himself, saying, 'What shall I do, since I have no room to store my crops?' So he said, 'I will do this: I will pull down my barns and build greater, and there I will store all my crops and my goods. And I will say to my soul, "Soul, you have many goods laid up for many years; take your ease; eat, drink, and be merry."' But God said to him, 'Fool! This night your soul will be required of you; then whose will those things be which you have provided?' "So is he who lays up treasure for himself, and is not rich toward God." Luke 12:15-21 (NKJV)

WHAT ARE WE COMMANDED BY THE TENTH COMMANDMENT?

We are commanded to trust God to direct our lives according His choosing. *"Trust in the Lord with all your heart, and lean not on your own understanding; In all your ways acknowledge Him, and He shall direct your paths."* Proverbs 3:5-6 (NKJV)

WHAT DOES THE TENTH COMMANDMENT FORBID?

It forbids all desire to take or keep unjustly anything that belongs to others. *"Woe to those who join house to house; they add field to field, till there is no place where they may dwell alone in the midst of the land!"* Isaiah 5:8 (NKJV)

"Woe to you, scribes and Pharisees, hypocrites! For you devour widows' houses, and for a pretense make long prayers. Therefore you will receive greater condemnation." Matthew 23:14 (NKJV)

"And having food and clothing, with these we shall be content. But those who desire to be rich fall into temptation and a snare, and into many foolish and harmful lusts which drown men in destruction and perdition. For the love of money is a root of all kinds of evil, for which some have strayed from the faith in their greediness, and pierced themselves through with many sorrows." 1 Timothy 6:8-10 (NKJV)

BIBLE NARRATIVES:

1) KING DAVID COVETED THE WIFE OF URIAH AND TOOK HER: 2 SAMUEL 11:2-4.
2) ABSALOM ESTRANGED THE HEARTS OF THE PEOPLE FROM DAVID BECAUSE HE COVETED DAVID'S THRONE: 2 SAMUEL 15:1-6.

3) BECAUSE JUDAS COVETED MONEY, HE BETRAYED JESUS CHRIST: MARK 14:10-11.

WHY DOES GOD FORBID COVETOUSNESS IN CHURCH LEADERS?

Covetous people will not work within the limits of their calling and as a result will bring division within the Church and will stop the flow of God's blessings. *"For this you know, that no fornicator, unclean person, nor covetous man, who is an idolater, has any inheritance in the kingdom of Christ and God."* Ephesians 5:5 (NKJV)

"A bishop then must be blameless, the husband of one wife, temperate, sober-minded, of good behavior, hospitable, able to teach; not given to wine, not violent, not greedy for money, but gentle, not quarrelsome, not covetous." 1 Timothy 3:2-3 (NKJV)

"Let each one remains in the same calling in which he was called." 1 Corinthians 7:20 (NKJV)

BIBLE NARRATIVES:

1) UZZIAH'S INTRUSION INTO THE PRIEST'S OFFICE HIS PUNISHMENT BY DEATH: 2 CHRONICLES 26
2) SIN OF KORAH, DOTHAM AND ABIRAM: NUMBERS 16

WHAT DOES GOD REQUIRE OF US IN THE TENTH COMMANDMENT?

God requires that we seek first the kingdom of God and His righteousness.

"But seek first the kingdom of God and His righteousness, and all these things shall be added to you." Matthew 6:33 (NKJV)

"Now godliness with contentment is great gain." 1 Timothy 6:6

WHAT ARE THE BENEFITS OF AVOIDING COVETOUSNESS?

We are given an inward peace and security knowing that our heavenly Father is aware of our needs and will take good care of us. *"Therefore I say to you, do not worry about your life, what you will eat or what you will drink; nor about your body, what you will put on. Is not life more than food and the body more than clothing? Look at the birds of the air, for they neither sow nor reap nor gather into barns; yet your heavenly Father feeds them. Are you not of more value than they? Which of you by worrying can add one cubit to his stature? "So why do you worry about clothing? Consider the lilies of the field, how they grow: they neither toil nor spin; and yet I say to you that even Solomon in all his glory was not arrayed like one of these. Now if God so clothes the grass of the field, which today is, and tomorrow is thrown into the oven, will He not much more clothe you, O you of little faith? "Therefore do not worry, saying, 'What shall we eat?' or 'What shall we drink?' or 'What shall we wear?' For after all these things the Gentiles seek. For your heavenly Father knows that you need all these things."* Matthew 6:25-32 (NKJV)

WHAT ARE SOME EXAMPLES OF COVETOUSNESS?

Examples of covetousness are gambling, greed, jealousy, envy, lust and selfishness.

WHY IS GAMBLING A BREAKING OF THE TENTH COMMANDMENT?

Coveting another man's goods and securing them by unlawful means and not by honest labor is breaking the tenth commandment.

WHY DOES GOD SAY *"THOU SHALT NOT"* IN THE ENTIRE TEN COMMANDMENTS?

Our heavenly Father desires our welfare and has lovingly listed the ten most dangerous traps Satan has set before our feet. He admonishes us..... *"Thou shalt not"* do these things if you want to be blessed with love, peace and happiness.

SUNDAY SCHOOL QUESTIONS

Q1. WHAT IS THE TENTH COMMANDMENT?
Q2. WHAT DOES COVET MEAN?
Q3. WHAT ARE WE COMMANDED BY THE TENTH COMMANDMENT?
Q4. WHAT DOES THE TENTH COMMANDMENT FORBID?
Q5. WHY DOES GOD FORBID COVETOUSNESS IN CHURCH LEADERS?
Q6. WHAT DOES GOD REQUIRE OF US IN THE TENTH COMMANDMENT?
Q7. WHAT ARE THE BENEFITS OF AVOIDING COVETOUSNESS?

Q8. WHAT ARE SOME EXAMPLES OF COVETOUSNESS?
Q9. WHY IS GAMBLING A BREAKING OF THE TENTH COMMANDMENT?
Q10. WHY DOES GOD SAY "THOU SHALT NOT" IN ALL THE COMMANDMENT?

Memory Verse: "Now godliness with contentment is great gain." 1 Timothy 6:6

Prayer: *O God Grant me the grace to keep Your Laws.*

The Word Today: Genesis 15:6-7 (NKJV)

"And he believed in the Lord, and He accounted it to him for righteousness. Then He said to him, "I am the Lord, who brought you out of Ur of the Chaldeans, to give you this land to inherit it."

I PROPHESY! GOD SHALL LEAD ME TO MY BREAKTHROUGH!

𝒢od is mindful of His children. His plan for you is to give you that which is good, even the best in life. So, as long, as you remain faithful to Him, you will always be increased miraculously. In Jeremiah 29:11, He said, *"I know the thoughts that I think toward you.., thoughts of peace, and not of evil, to give you an expected end."*

So, what is it you desire? Is it a car, a house, life partner, child, wealth etc? Whatever it is, receive it now in Jesus' name. Amen!

God does not call a person in vain. Before he called Abraham, He had set aside possessions for him, as soon as Abraham obeyed Him; he stepped into his breakthrough; like He did for Abraham He will do for you. God has set aside some possessions for you. All you need do is to find out what He wants you to do and how He wants you to do it. As soon as you discover that and begin to work towards it, the provisions He has made available for you to accomplish the mission will begin to present themselves to you. Do you desire to step into your breakthrough? Then say this prayer loud and clear:

Prayer: *Lord, I thank you for giving Your life for my sake on the cross of Calvary. Today, I give and rededicate my life to You now. Lead and direct me to my breakthrough in Jesus' name. Amen!*

The Word Today: Psalm 69:30

"I will praise the name of God with a song, and will magnify him with thanksgiving."

I RECEIVE THE GRACE TO APPRECIATE THE LORD GOD!

John Piper said *"Friends, let us reflect and live a life which exalts the supremacy of God in all things. The ultimate purpose of our lives is to glorify God and enjoy Him forever."* Thanksgiving is the act of giving thanks: it is a prayer expressing gratitude; it is expressing a feeling of being thankful to somebody for doing something. The Hebrew word for "thanksgiving" is "TOWDAH" meaning confessing, praise and thanksgiving. The Greek word for "thanksgiving" is "EUCHARISTA" meaning thankfulness or the giving of thanks. Thanksgiving always has to do with showing gratitude for something the Lord God has done for you or something you are expecting God to do for you by faith. You thank God also for sending His Son to die for you, for healing you, for delivering you, for meeting your all needs, etc. So get to it now and give thanks to God!

PRAYER OF THANKSGIVING:

Father! Thank You for last year, Thank You for what You did last month, last week, thank You for yesterday. I thank You Lord in advance for what You will yet do for me and my loved ones. Thank You for Salvation of soul. Thank You for Healing and deliverance, thank You for Anointing, thank You for power and authority, thank You for breakthrough; thank You, for fighting my battles for me. Thank You for giving me victory. O Lord I appreciate You. I give You all the glory, honor and adoration Lord! May You forever be glorified! Thank You O God of heaven. Thank You Almighty God! Accept my thanks in Jesus' name!

December 31ˢᵗ

The Word Today: Psalm 65:11 (AKJV)

"You crown the year with your goodness; and your paths drop fatness."

GOD SHALL CROWN MY YEAR WITH GOONESS OF FATNESS!

1.   I declare the lord God shall cause "the clouds to pour down their moisture and abundant showers on me and my loved ones." Job 36:28.

2.   I declare the Lord God shall make me lie down in green pastures, and lead me beside still waters." Psalm 23:2.

3.   I declare the Lord shall satisfy me... "When I give to them, they gather it up; when I open my hand, I am satisfied with good things." Psalm 104:28

4.   I declare... the Lord shall grants unto me peace in my borders and satisfies me with the finest of wheat. Psalm 147:14

5.   I declare... the Lord shall "crown the year for me with His goodness; and drop fatness on my paths" Psalm 65:11 (AKJV)

6.   I declare... the Lord shall grant me abundance, and Crown me with glory. He shall crown the year end with fatness on my pathway, goodness and long Life upon me, He shall rain on me financial abundance this year end and the year to come in Jesus' mighty name. Amen! Glory to God!

PRAYER POINTS:

1. *Every power attacking my calling and testimonies at the Battle of the gates: die by Fire in the name of Jesus. Amen!*

2. *Every dark conspiracy to abort my victory at the battle of the gate, scatter unto desolation in the name of Jesus.*

3. *Every satanic gang-up assigned to abort my testimonies at this Battle of the gates: you are a failure, die by fire.*

4. *I soak this Battle of the gates prayer in the blood of Jesus.*

5. *The gates of hell shall not prevail against me in Jesus' name.*

5. *Powers of delay, assigned to hinder my testimonies in the New Year crumble to dust and be blown away by the wind of the Holy Ghost into the valley of failure and disgrace in Jesus' name.*

6. *Stars from Heaven, Fight my battles for me after the order of Barak and Deborah in the name of Jesus. Amen!*

7. *Every enemy army arrayed in battle against my destiny this New Year: Hear the Verdict of fire perish in battle in Jesus' name.*

8. *Every satanic archer targeting my prayer life this New Year: Catch Fire and Burn to ashes in the name of Jesus. Amen!*

9. *Arrows of weariness, frustration and failure, fired against me at my altar of prayer: backfire back to senders in Jesus' name.*

10. *O God Arise and let Your Fear and Dread fall upon every of my enemy at the battle of the gates, in Jesus' name.*

11. *Holy Ghost Fire! Rekindle my prayer fire unto victories in the battle of the gates prayer session, in the name of Jesus. Amen!*

12. *Every holy warrior fighting at the Battle of the gates, receive fresh surge of Fire to prevail at the altar of prayer.*

Dear Father,
I come to You in the Name of Jesus. Your Word says in John 6:37 *"...him that cometh to me, I will in no wise cast out"*.
 I thank You for not casting me out. I thank You for drawing me onto You, I surrender my life to You today and I confess with my mouth that Jesus Christ is Lord and I believe with my heart that you raised Him from the dead. I ask that the blood of Jesus cleanse me from all my sin and deliver me from all my iniquity Thank You Lord for saving me. Father, please write my name in the book of life in Jesus name I pray. Amen

Heavens are rejoicing this day for your sake.

Name: ....

Address: ....

....

Contact number: ....

Date: ....

JOIN THE INTERNATIONAL PROPHETIC PRAYER CONFERENCE

DIAL 712.432.0075 AND ENTER CODE 188641#

6AM AND 10 PM EST

MONDAYS THROUGH SATURDAYS; 5PM ONLY ON SUNDAYS.
CALL TOLL TO FREE TO ORDER FOR PRAYERS
1.800.481 3884 FAX PRAYERS TO 1.888. 412.5006

E-MAIL PRAYER REQUEST, DREAM INTERPRETATIONS AND TESTIMONIES TO
oracleprophetess@gmail.com

For more information or to donate and support the work God is doing in
Oracle of God Ministries International

ORACLE OF GOD INTERNATIONAL MINISTRIES

***An International Full Gospel and Deliverance, Prayer
and Prophetic Ministry***
URL: www.oogod.org/ www.oracleofgodmnistries.net/
E-Mail: *pastor@oogod.org donate@oracleofgodministries.net/*
P. O. BOX 14068 RALEIGH NC 27620.
TEL: 1800.481.3884. FAX: 1888.413.5990
PRAYER CONFERENCE: 267.507.0240 ENTER 605815
MONDAYS THROUGH SATURDAYS @ 6 AM AND 10 PM EST